CARRIE LEVIN

and

ANN NICKINSON

ILLUSTRATIONS
BY
ABBY CARTER

A Fireside Book Published by
Simon & Schuster, Inc. New York

GOOD

Bountiful

ENOUGH

Home Cooking

TO EAT

A Fireside Book,
Published by Simon & Schuster, Inc.
Simon & Schuster Building
Rockefeller Center
1230 Avenue of the Americas
New York, New York 10020
FIRESIDE and colophon are registered trademarks of Simon & Schuster, Inc.
Good Enough to Eat is a trademark of
Good Enough to Eat, Inc.

Designed by Bonni Leon

Manufactured in the United States of America
1   3   5   7   9   10   8   6   4   2
Library of Congress Cataloging in Publication Data
Levin, Carrie.
Good Enough to Eat.

"A Fireside book."
Includes index.
1. Cookery, American.   2. Menus.   I. Nickinson, Ann.
II. Good Enough to Eat, Inc. (Manhattan, New York, N.Y.)
III. Title.
TX715.L6595   1987   641.5'09747'1   86-29419
ISBN: 0-671-62554-3

Acknowledgments

To our families and friends, who always knew we could do it.
To Bill Perley, a constant and staunch support. To Jill
Bobigan, for always being there for everything.
Chef Seppi Renggli for teaching Carrie to respect food in all its
states, and for glorifying home cooking.
Abby Carter, whose pictures speak louder than words.
Ricky Braunshweiger, our butcher, for being a great shoulder to
lean on and for providing financial and emotional suppport.
The Selch family for room and board.
Susie Skolnick for being part of the beginning.
Ruth Coran Sholes for her talent and inspiration.
Mario Sartori for getting the ball rolling and for being a good
friend.
Sandy Greeley, who helped turn dreams into words.
James Chen, a new member of our family.
Chris Tomasino, who helped us win our battles.
Joan Michelle for her help in editing.
Cathy Hemming, Tim McGinnis, Laura Yorke, Nancy Kalish,
Carole Lalli, Eve Metz, Bonni Leon and everybody else at
Simon and Schuster.
And, from the bottom of our hearts, to all those special and
talented people at Good Enough to Eat restaurants. To the
present and past people who have made us proud, we thank you.
Concetta Tedesco, Keith Kriha, Karina Nielsen, Jill Bernstein,
Joe Loftis, Lisa Hall, Judy Nikolai, Jenny Lee, Alex Danyluk,
Peter Landroche, Jon Naberezny, Jodie Trapani, Lee Duberman,
Maura Rankin, Stripe Grapentin-Benedict, Lilly Chance and
of course, Ginnie Mae.

To the
fun of making
and eating
food

C O N T

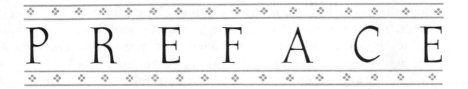

ny meal at Good Enough to Eat conjures up some indelible images of an earlier, quieter America when families ate together. A farmhand's heaping plate. The squeaky front-porch swing. Grandma sloshing the butter churner. Egg-washed loaves cooling on a sunny windowsill. Tanned youngsters picking berries from the family patch. A neighbor's dog chasing the marmalade cat. Honeysuckle, pansies, rambler roses . . .

How have we two young women chefs managed to recreate that in Manhattan's glitz and frenzy? We have stuck to our dreams of serving forth homey foods, childhood nostalgia, and country abundance to city folk more attuned and accustomed to *nouvelle* polish than blue-plate specials. We have insisted on the wood-topped tables, heavy pottery, burly napkins, and fresh country flowers more suited to a family dining room than a city restaurant. We have staffed Good Enough to Eat with cooks, bakers, and waiters who share our extended-family concept of cooking and eating.

But it's the food that draws the customers, tired of trendy, and wistful for home-cooked meals. Comforting. Peasanty. Kids' food with ketchup. The meals are all that, but more. They are also shaded with French, Belgian, and Jewish overtones that somehow work, without contradicting the premise of American farm meals.

The result, we often say, is chic food from homespun ingredients. The gray flannel suit of restaurant food, slightly sophisticated and durable. For after all, what was honest and presentable twenty years ago is now, and shall be so, twenty years hence. With food, you can always go home again. Customers must agree—Good Enough to Eat has expanded from a tearoom and catering service into two major Manhattan restaurants.

Despite our markedly different backgrounds—Carrie was raised in Belgium, Ann grew up in Boston—we share common culinary goals and tastes. We think about foods all the time, always dreaming up something new. As homey and honest as our meals are, they spring from a mingling of Old and New World ideas, and several unexpected culinary threads bind them together: the sweet-savory tastes beloved by Jewish home cooks; the crunchy outside–mushy inside textures that have a beguiling, innocent appeal; the deft ethnic seasonings that pique the taste buds; the mounded plates that tempt limp appetites. Waiters balance plates at eye level, and what hungry customers see gliding past is layered abundance, stirring appetites for, and memories of, Thanksgiving feasts. There's a tiered appearance to the mounded plates—slices of meat accented by an artful pile of vegetables, so that nothing is one level. It's an exacting look, but without being exact.

A perfection within an imperfection.

To make these wonderful dishes taste just as good as they appear, we stress the importance of reading recipes thoroughly. Before cooking begins, know what ingredients and utensils are required. Think through a time schedule so that all parts of the meal will be ready simultaneously, because a meal should be both satisfying and calming, and one served with long intervals between courses will not have that effect.

We believe a kitchen should be well stocked, and to make all the recipes in this book we suggest having the following on hand: kosher salt and olive oil; seasonings: black and white pepper, sage,  cayenne, paprika, dry mustard, oregano, thyme, basil, rosemary, cinnamon, nutmeg, pure vanilla extract; condiments: Worcestershire sauce, soy sauce, wine, hot sauce; utensils: tongs, stockpot, small and medium saucepan, grater, chopping board, an 8-inch and a 10-inch skillet, slotted spoon, wooden spoon, sieve, colander, cast-iron

I

MORNING MEALS

A s no other meal, breakfast and brunch should waken the senses. For that matter, no other meal can really match breakfast and brunch for beguiling aromas— freshly baked blueberry muffins, perking coffee, salty bacon, peppery hash browns crisping in butter, waffles steaming in an iron. No other meal mingles such flavors—the sweetness of whipped strawberry butter on warm buttermilk biscuits, or rum-spiked poached peaches ladled over cinnamony French toast, or nutty Brie folded with tart strawberries into a creamy omelet. No other meal can be as visual—stacks of golden pancakes glistening with melted butter and amber syrup, or pale yellow scrambled eggs speckled with freshly ground black pepper, or a bowl of multi-textured granola adorned with carefully pared fresh fruit.

Breakfast and brunch are truly wonderful, fun, memorable meals. Served in a homey setting—red-checked tablecloth, a pitcher of fresh daisies, soft cloth napkins, butter spooned into ramekins, casual but colorful pottery—they should immediately connote happy families sharing laughter and warm  hearts—perhaps even the family cat curled up on a calico cushion, or Aunt Martha scooping up second helpings of raspberries and cream.

Sadly, breakfasts and brunches are often the most neglected meals at the American table. Even on weekends when people do have the time, too many rush through what should be a leisurely sit-down meal, wholesome and comforting. Maybe breakfast and brunch foods seem too complex to fuss with, but we assure you they are not.

As we have discovered at Good Enough to Eat, most people really do love a robust morning meal served in a homey atmosphere. In fact, we began our restaurant by offering just breakfast foods from early morning to late afternoon when we closed. Customers lined up for an hour or more on weekends and holidays, even standing in a snowstorm or wilting heat, to enjoy these meals. They still do.

 Every day of the week we continue to serve real old-fashioned, country-style American breakfasts and brunches—all foods we love to eat ourselves, and which most restaurants don't offer. Our portions are heaping, too, just like you might find at a farm table or a country inn, and enough food to make this your main meal of the day. Also, we believe so much in breakfast foods that if in mid-afternoon a hungry customer craves scrambled eggs with biscuits and strawberry butter or apple pancakes with sugar-cured bacon rather than a sandwich or soup, we will serve these dishes.

Our sweets and extras—moist blueberry muffins, rich coffee cakes, buttermilk biscuits, sugar-cured bacon, golden hash browns, and whipped fruit butters—put the finishing touches on these glorious meals.

Breakfast and Brunch Recipes

GRANOLA

10 cups old-fashioned rolled oats
 3 cups flaked coconut
 1 cup sesame seeds
 1 cup mixed nuts—walnuts, pecans and almonds
2½ tablespoons ground cinnamon
 ¾ teaspoon ground nutmeg
 1 teaspoon salt
1¼ cups sweet butter, melted
1¼ cups honey
 ½ cup chopped dates
 ½ cup chopped figs
 ½ cup apricots
 1 cup golden raisins

Preheat oven to 350 degrees.

Combine oats, coconut, seeds, nuts, spices and salt in a large mixing bowl. In a smaller bowl, mix the butter and honey together, then drizzle over the mixture. Then mix oats mixture and honey-butter mixture together by hand until moist, but do not overwork. Press this ½ inch thick onto sheets and place in oven. Bake for 15 minutes, or until golden. With spatula, turn mixture over in large chunks. Bake other side 5 minutes, taking care not to burn.

Remove from the sheets and put mixture into bowls, breaking into bite-sized chunks. Stir in the fruits. When completely cooled, place mixture in airtight containers and store in a cool place.

POACHED EGGS ON DILL BREAD

P oached eggs are easy to cook successfully if you use ultra-fresh eggs so the yolks stay centered in the white and so the eggs won't disintegrate in hot water. To prepare poached eggs, fill a small saucepan with water (with a pinch of salt added) and bring the water to a vigorous boil. Then turn the heat down until the water is simmering. Crack an egg into the center of the water and turn the flame down until the water is still. Allow the egg to cook for 2 to 3 minutes, being sure it never sticks to the pan. Carefully remove it with a slotted spoon, patting the spoon bottom with a paper towel to blot up extra water. Slide the egg onto toasted, buttered Dill Bread (recipe below), or whatever toast you prefer. If you wish, cook two eggs at the same time.

For more tips on poaching, see page 69.

DILL BREAD

  2 packages dried yeast
     pinch of sugar
 ½ cup warm water
 ¾ cup milk
 ¾ cup cottage cheese
  1 tablespoon honey
1½ teaspoons salt
  3 tablespoons sweet butter, softened or melted
  5 cups all-purpose flour
 ¼ cup fresh dill, minced
 ½ cup onion, finely chopped
  1 whole egg beaten with 1 tablespoon water for wash

dill

Dissolve the yeast in the water with a pinch of sugar to help the yeast react, leaving it until the yeast foams. Meanwhile, in a saucepan, heat the milk, cottage cheese, honey, salt and butter, until lukewarm. Put 4 cups of flour into a large mixing bowl. When the milk mixture is warmed, add the dill and onion to it, stirring well to combine. Then add the yeast mixture to the milk, blending well. Stir this into the flour. Add the remaining flour, and stir to make a soft, sticky dough. Put this dough into a greased bowl, cover with a clean damp towel and set in a warm spot to rise and double, for about 1 hour.

Preheat the oven to 350 degrees. Punch the risen dough down, and divide it in half. Grease well 2 eight-inch loaf pans, and put half the dough into each pan. Brush tops of loaves with the egg wash, then let them rise until double in volume. Bake for 40 minutes, remove from the oven and cool on racks.

HOLE IN THE BREAD

SERVES

1

*T*his unusual buttery, fried egg–bread combination brings back childhood memories, when weekends meant "hole-in-the-bread." Some people eat the "round" by itself first; others dunk it into the yolk, reserving this particular treat till the last.

  2 slices bread per person
  2 tablespoons butter, melted
  2 eggs per person

Cut out a 1-inch round from the center of each slice of bread. With 2 tablespoons melted butter, grease a griddle or skillet, and brush butter on both sides of the "round" and the bread slices and brown one side. Flip the slices and the round and crack an egg into the hole in the center. After 40 seconds again flip over the egg, the slices, and the cut-out round with a spatula, and cook another 40 seconds. Serve by capping the egg with the toasted round.

griddle, muffin tins, 9-inch cake tins, tube pan, bundt pan, sauce-pan for deep-fat frying, roaster, 1 rectangular, 1 square and 1 round ovenproof baking dish, cookie sheets, steel for sharpening knives, nesting stainless mixing bowls, parchment paper, slotted and regular spatula, palette knife, rubber spatula, pastry brush, baster, stainless whisk, rolling pin, measuring cups and spoons, the convenience of a food processor or blender (although we cooked for a year, serving 200 customers daily, without either appliance).

Our greatest joy is to pretend that we are mothers at home cooking for loads of relatives and friends. And then we stand back and watch how everyone enjoys the food.

Carrie Levin
Ann Nickinson

Scrambled Eggs

We believe that most people have never really tasted properly prepared scrambled eggs: they are usually overcooked and dried out. For creamy, moist scrambled eggs—the way we think they should be eaten—select fresh extra-large eggs and crack three of them per person into a high narrow container, such as a measuring cup. You want the beating perimeter narrow to avoid incorporating air. You just want to make the eggs frothy, and to mix the whites well with the yolks. The whites cook more quickly than the yolks, and unless they are well incorporated, they will leave streaks that ribbon through the cooked scrambled eggs. Beat the eggs in a rotary movement using your wrists so you hit all sides of the cup. Don't add milk to the beaten eggs or they will become heavy and stick to the pan.

Use a heavy-bottomed, well-seasoned skillet for cooking. Add 2 tablespoons melted clarified butter and heat the butter over medium heat, but don't let it brown or smoke. To test for proper butter temperature, dribble some beaten egg off the prongs of the fork into the pan. If the egg coagulates immediately, the pan is ready. Pour the eggs into the pan. Right away, they start to form a cooked coagulation on the sides. Use the side of a fork to pull the cooking eggs toward you from the far side. Go around the pan, pulling the eggs into the center and circling around the center. When the eggs are ready to serve, they will still be ripply and wet on top. Of course, if you want firmer eggs, keep on pulling the wet eggs into the center until they cook through. You don't want the eggs to brown, however; this means they have over-cooked and will be tough. If you wish, sprinkle cheese on at the last moment, then fork the eggs out and serve.

✿ ✿ ✿ ✿ ✿ ✿ ✿ ✿ ✿ ✿ ✿ ✿ ✿ ✿ ✿

APPLE PANCAKES WITH POACHED APPLE TOPPING

SERVES
4

Our adaptable pancake batter—a thick, wholesome mixture that satisfies the hungriest appetites—was devised as an experiment in taste combinations. We combined various flours and grains for texture and nutrition. The result is a batter heartier than one made with all white flour, but lighter than one of only whole-wheat flour. We find the oatmeal keeps it moist.

We happen to love these pancakes, perfect for a fall breakfast, because the sugar in the apples caramelizes and produces a wonderful taste.

But we wanted the batter to be a good backdrop for a variety of fillings. It will suit whatever ingredients you have on hand—blueberries cooked cranberries, sliced peaches, etc. But whatever filling you use, don't add it to the batter. Instead, sprinkle it on top of batter after 1 minute. You don't want the filling to hit the heat first, but to be buffered by the cooked side of the pancake. Butter the

griddle before you begin, but never butter
it between pancakes or they won't brown
evenly. When the pancake starts to bubble
around the edges, lift up an edge with a
spatula and peek underneath to see if the
underside is turning golden. If so, flip it.
But if you turn a pancake too soon, the
uncooked batter will ooze out on the skillet. Turn pancakes only once.

¼ cup sweet butter, melted
3 cups buttermilk
4 extra-large eggs
¾ cup plus 1 tablespoon all-purpose flour
¼ cup whole-wheat flour
¼ cup wheat germ
¼ cup rolled oats
1 tablespoon cornmeal
1½ teaspoons baking powder
½ teaspoon baking soda
1 teaspoon sugar
 pinch of salt
1 apple, peeled, cored, and sliced in very thin wedges

In a large mixing bowl, whisk together butter, buttermilk, and
eggs. Combine the flours, wheat germ, oats, cornmeal, baking
powder, baking soda, sugar, and salt in a separate bowl. Make a
well in center, and pour in buttermilk mixture; stir to combine but
do not overbeat or the pancakes will be tough. Allow batter to relax
15 to 20 minutes.

To make pancakes, butter and preheat skillet or griddle. For
each pancake, ladle on 1 cup batter, and top with apple wedges
spoke-fashion in center. Cook about 4 minutes, until bottom is
golden and bubbles appear on pancake, then turn with spatula and
cook about 4 minutes longer, until golden on second side. Remove
pancake apple side up to plate and cover with a bowl to keep
moist. Repeat with remaining batter and apples to make 4 pancakes.

Peeling and cutting fruits are simple procedures, but ones to know since fruits are used in such a large variety of recipes. Here are our helpful hints on cutting and peeling apples: To peel from top to bottom, use a sharp peeler or a knife to cut around the fruit in a circle. Then slice the apple in half lengthwise, then into quarters. Remove the core and the ends, and cut into even ⅛-inch-thick slices.

TOPPING

  1 cup sour cream
     Poached Apple Topping (recipe follows)
     cinnamon sugar to taste

POACHED APPLE TOPPING

  ¾ cup firmly packed brown sugar
  ⅓ cup honey
  1 tablespoon lemon juice
  ¼ teaspoon ground cinnamon
  ¼ cup apple cider
  ¼ cup raisins, or to taste
  3 apples

MAKES
ABOUT
2 CUPS

Place sugar, honey, lemon juice, cinnamon and cider in saucepan over low heat, and, holding the pan by its handle, swirl continuously without stirring, to prevent sugar from crystallizing. When sugar has dissolved, raise heat and simmer for 5 minutes. Add raisins and continue cooking over low heat.

Meanwhile, peel, core, and slice apples into ⅛-inch-thick pieces. When liquid is thick and syrupy and coats the back of a spoon (after about 15 minutes), add the apples. Turn the heat down as low as possible, and poach the apples until they are soft but still retain their shape, about 10 minutes longer.

To serve, spoon a portion of sour cream over each pancake and surround it with a portion of Poached Apple Topping. Sprinkle with cinnamon sugar.

BANANA WALNUT PANCAKES

*U*se the same basic batter as for Apple Pancakes, allowing enough batter—about 1⅓ cups per person—to make 3 large pancakes per person. Ladle the batter onto the griddle, then sprinkle 2 teaspoons chopped walnuts evenly over top of each pancake. After flipping the pancakes, peel and slice 1 banana per person. Remove the pancakes from the griddle and arrange the banana slices on the pancakes, sprinkling the stack with extra walnuts, if you wish.

CHOCOLATE WAFFLES WITH ALMOND BUTTER

SERVES
4

*W*affles have become a morning classic at Good Enough to Eat. Our first waffle effort, however, was disastrous. Neither of us admitted to the other that we had never made a waffle before. We plugged in our new machine—we always use a Belgian waffle maker because we love the deep ridges it produces—and as it heated up, we noticed a strange aroma. We had left the instructions inside. Then, after removing the burned instructions and cleaning the iron, we added too much batter, and, of course, it oozed out. We tried again with more batter, and opened the machine too soon, while it was still steaming: the waffle was raw. That was the end of waffles for that day. Our advice: Read—and follow—the manufacturer's instructions for waffle making that come with each iron.

3 cups all-purpose flour
2 tablespoons baking powder
2 tablespoons sugar
2 teaspoons salt
6 large eggs, lightly beaten
3 cups milk
3 tablespoons cocoa, unsweetened
¾ cup sweet butter, melted

SUGAR TOPPING

½ cup sifted powdered
   sugar
2 tablespoons cocoa,
   unsweetened

GARNISH

½ cup almonds, slivered
   and toasted
1 cup strawberries,
   cleaned and hulled

ALMOND BUTTER

½ cup almonds, slivered and toasted
1 cup sweet butter, softened
¼ teaspoon almond extract
1 teaspoon dark rum

✿ ✿ ✿ ✿ ✿ ✿ ✿ ✿ ✿ ✿ ✿ ✿ ✿ ✿

To roast nuts, lay them on a baking sheet, and roast them for 10 minutes, with no added oil or salt, in a 350-degree oven. During the cooking time, flip them once with a spatula.

✿ ✿ ✿ ✿ ✿ ✿ ✿ ✿ ✿ ✿ ✿ ✿ ✿ ✿

Combine the flour, baking powder, sugar, cocoa, and salt together in a mixing bowl. Make a well in the dry ingredients, and pour the eggs, milk, and butter in the center. Slowly whip the ingredients together, taking care not to overmix the batter so it does not become tough. If a few lumps remain, don't worry. Cover the mixing bowl and put it in the refrigerator for half an hour to relax the batter.

Meanwhile, for the topping, combine the powdered sugar and the 2 tablespoons cocoa in a small bowl and set aside.

Prepare the Almond Butter. Roast all the almonds on a cookie sheet until they turn golden, about 6 to 8 minutes, in a 350-degree oven. Place ½ cup almonds in the work bowl of a food processor and pulverize. Add the cup of sweet butter, the almond extract and the rum and process until smooth. Reserve the remaining ½ cup almonds for garnish.

Heat the waffle iron. Remove the batter from the refrigerator, and when the iron is ready, cook the batter according to manufacturer's instructions. About 6 to 8 ounces of batter are necessary for each waffle. Usually waffles are ready when they stop steaming. Remove the whole waffle from the iron, and separate along the grooved iron markings. Place separated waffles overlapping on the serving plate, topping each with a spoonful of almond butter. Garnish each waffle with a spoonful of reserved toasted almonds and sliced strawberries, then sprinkle the sugar-cocoa mixture on top.

FRENCH TOAST

SERVES 4

We tried many different recipes till we found just the right French toast. For our tastes, thickly sliced day-old bread works best because it acts like a sponge, soaking up the egg mixture without crumbling. When cooked, the outsides are crusty and the insides custardy. We always use our Cinnamon Swirl Bread, but you can use any textured bread, like challah or Italian, as long as it soaks up the egg mixture really well.

  1 loaf Cinnamon Swirl Bread (recipe on page 28)
  6 large eggs
1½ cups milk
  ½ teaspoon vanilla extract
    pinch of salt
  4 tablespoons sweet butter, melted

TOPPING

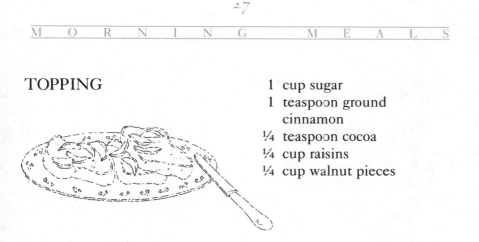

1 cup sugar
1 teaspoon ground
  cinnamon
¼ teaspoon cocoa
¼ cup raisins
¼ cup walnut pieces

Cut the bread into ¾-inch slices, allowing 3 slices per person. Combine the eggs, milk, vanilla extract and salt in a mixing bowl, beating well. Dunk the bread slices in this mixture for about 3 minutes, or until the slices are soaked through.

Place a skillet or griddle over medium-high heat and brush its surface with 2 tablespoons of the butter. Place as many slices as will fit without crowding in the skillet, and brush the top surface of each slice with more melted butter to seal in the egg. Lower the heat, and cook each slice 7 minutes on each side; when the bread puffs up like a soufflé, it's ready. Don't push it down.

While the slices are cooking, prepare the topping mixture. In a mixing bowl combine the sugar, cinnamon and cocoa, stirring well. Add the raisins and nuts. Place French toast on heated plates (or a large serving platter) and sprinkle top of each slice with this crunchy mixture to serve.

✧ ✧ ✧ ✧ ✧ ✧ ✧ ✧ ✧ ✧ ✧ ✧ ✧ ✧ ✧

We love to use strawberries in our meals, either as main components or as garnishes. Select plump, unblemished ones, and rinse them in cold water, leaving the stems on. To prepare for garnish, take a sharp paring knife, lift up the edges of the leaves, and, right next to where the stem attaches to the berry, slice in half lengthwise.

✧ ✧ ✧ ✧ ✧ ✧ ✧ ✧ ✧ ✧ ✧ ✧ ✧ ✧ ✧

PEACH OR STRAWBERRY TOPPING

SERVES
4

  1 recipe French Toast (page 26)
½ cup rum
½ cup sugar
  1 teaspoon lemon juice
½ peach, cut into thin wedges, or 5 strawberries, hulled and thinly sliced

Put the rum, sugar and lemon juice in a small saucepan over low heat, swirling until the sugar dissolves. Bring the mixture to a slow boil until it reduces in volume by ⅓. Add the sliced fruit and lower the heat, cooking 5 to 10 minutes to soften. If you wish, you can substitute any fruit juice with a little water for the rum.

CINNAMON SWIRL BREAD

  1 cup milk
  2 packages dried yeast
¼ cup sugar
  4 tablespoons sweet butter, melted
  1 teaspoon salt
  4 cups all-purpose flour
  2 large eggs
  1 tablespoon water
⅓ cup sugar, mixed with 2 teaspoons cinnamon

Heat the milk to lukewarm in a saucepan over medium heat. Remove from the heat. Pour ¼ cup of the milk into a small bowl. Add the 2 packages of yeast and allow the yeast to dissolve and foam.

Pour the remaining milk into a large mixing bowl, and to this add the sugar, melted butter and salt. In a separate bowl, place 2 cups of the flour and add the proofed yeast. Gradually stir in the milk mixture. When all the ingredients are well blended, stir in 1 egg, and the remaining flour.

Scoop the dough cut onto a floured surface. Knead 10 minutes, or until the dough becomes a silky, cohesive mass. Butter a mixing bowl and put the dough into it, turning to coat the entire surface. Cover the dough with a clean towel, set in a warm spot, and let it rise until double in bulk, about 1 hour.

Punch the dough down, divide it in half, and let it rest for about 10 minutes. Meanwhile, prepare an egg wash with the remaining egg and 1 tablespoon water. Butter 2 loaf pans approximately 5½ by 8½ inches. On a floured surface, roll each dough portion out into a rectangle, about 8 inches by 12 inches. Brush the dough with egg wash, then sprinkle with the cinnamon sugar. Roll up each rectangle jelly-roll fashion, and place them in the prepared pans. Brush again with remaining egg wash. Let the loaves rise again. Preheat the oven to 350 degrees, and when the loaves are nearly doubled in size (in about 45 minutes), place them in the oven and bake for 40 minutes. The loaves are done when the sides and bottoms are golden brown. Turn the loaves out onto racks to cool.

✿ ✿ ✿ ✿ ✿ ✿ ✿ ✿ ✿ ✿ ✿ ✿ ✿ ✿ ✿

Studying omelet making has been an obsession of ours. If you can master this technique, you are mastering one of the greatest feats in cooking. You may have to make many omelets before you get the hang of them, but don't get discouraged because they are worth the effort.

We have sampled numerous omelets in the United States, and even when we ask for an undercooked omelet, we are usually served a rubberized, overcooked mess. What we prefer, and teach how to make, are the runny, gooey, almost dribbly, omelets like the French and Belgians prepare. These omelets are fluffy and wrinkly on the outside, but not browned.

There's a structural difference, of course, between scrambled eggs and omelets, but, as with scrambled eggs, you want the omelet to have only the pure egg taste unadulterated by added water, milk or cream.

(continued on next page)

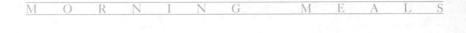

For adding cheese to omelets, pregrate the cheese on the large-holed side of a grater, or julienne the cheese so you can add it quickly while the omelet cooks. Don't chunk the cheese, because then it will not melt evenly into the eggs.

In a circular motion, beat 3 extra-large eggs in a small cup, as you do for scrambled eggs. Make 30 to 40 rotations with a fork. Using a small, well-seasoned skillet, or preferably an omelet pan, add 2 tablespoons of melted clarified butter. Heat the butter, and test for proper temperature by dribbling beaten egg into the pan, as with scrambled eggs. Once the butter is at the correct temperature, pour the beaten eggs in. Grasp the handle of the skillet, and tilt it away from you while simultaneously pulling the eggs up toward you with the prongs of a fork, letting the uncooked eggs run out around the fork. Reverse the tilting motion, and pull the eggs away from you. Repeat the first step, and when the eggs start to mound in the center, sprinkle on the cheese, if using. Repeat the pulling action until most of egg is cooked but still is runny and moist. Tilt the pan, slide the omelet onto your warmed plate, folding it in half as you do so. If properly cooked, the omelet will have folds rippling across its moist surface, which means you have pulled the eggs often enough from one side of the pan to the other. This whole process takes only 30 seconds. You may even want to cook it a second or two less because the omelet continues to cook once it is folded over on the serving plate.

PROVENÇAL OMELET

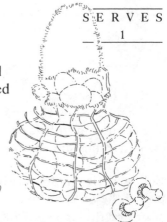

SERVES 1

- 3 extra-large eggs
- 2 tablespoons clarified butter, melted
- 2 fresh mushrooms, cleaned and sliced
- 2 to 3 tablespoons grated Gruyère
- 2 canned artichoke hearts, quartered
- 3 cherry tomatoes, halved
- 2 black olives, halved
  chopped parsley for garnish

Beat the eggs thoroughly, and heat the butter in an omelet pan or skillet. Add the sliced mushrooms, and sauté them for about a minute, shaking the pan so the mushrooms do not stick.

Dribble a little beaten egg into the pan to test butter temperature. When it is hot enough, pour in the eggs immediately and cook, following the above instructions for making an omelet. Add the grated Gruyère once the eggs begin to mound in the center of the pan, and continue the tilting motion to cook the eggs. Add the artichoke hearts and tomatoes, flip the omelet over, then pour it onto a warmed plate. Garnish with the olives and parsley.

✿ ✿ ✿ ✿ ✿ ✿ ✿ ✿ ✿ ✿ ✿ ✿ ✿ ✿

To season an omelet pan, the easiest and best method, which you can repeat, should your pan lose its nonsticking qualities, is to cover the surface of the pan with vegetable oil and a sprinkling of salt. Set over medium heat, then turn up to high until the oil smokes and the salt blackens. Remove the pan from the heat, and when the oil has cooled slightly, take a wad of paper towels held firmly between tongs, and scrub the bottom of the pan. Never substitute butter for the oil because it overheats too quickly.

✿ ✿ ✿ ✿ ✿ ✿ ✿ ✿ ✿ ✿ ✿ ✿ ✿ ✿

BRIE AND STRAWBERRY OMELET

SERVES
1

 3 extra-large eggs
 2 tablespoons clarified butter, melted
 3 ounces firm Brie (rind removed if you wish), julienned
 3 medium strawberries, rinsed, dried and thinly sliced

Follow basic omelet-making directions. Add the Brie after the first pull of the fork, making sure it is evenly scattered throughout. Add the strawberries after the second pull. Continue cooking according to directions.

✿ ✿ ✿ ✿ ✿ ✿ ✿ ✿ ✿ ✿ ✿ ✿ ✿ ✿ ✿ ✿

We always use triple A sweet butter because we bake so much, and sweet butter tastes better in baked goods. To clarify butter, melt over very low heat without burning, allowing it to separate naturally. The milk solids, which cause butter to burn, separate out and sink to the bottom of the liquefied butter. Skim off the white foam on top and save it for flavoring—then pour off the yellow layer (the clarified part) from the residue. Discard residue. Always use clarified butter for high-heat cooking, such as sautéing or, as used here, in omelet making.

✿ ✿ ✿ ✿ ✿ ✿ ✿ ✿ ✿ ✿ ✿ ✿ ✿ ✿ ✿ ✿

SAUSAGE AND POTATO OMELET

SERVES
1

 1 link breakfast sausage, cut into rounds
 1 new potato, cooked
 2 tablespoons clarified butter, melted
 3 extra-large eggs
 2 tablespoons Gruyère, grated, optional

Cut the sausage and potato into ¼-inch rounds. Then slice the potato rounds in half. Put the butter in the pan and heat it, then add the sausage and potato and cook for 2 to 3 minutes, shaking the pan constantly. Add the eggs, beaten, and follow the basic omelet-making directions. If you wish, add the cheese after the first pull of the fork.

BACON-LETTUCE-TOMATO OMELET

SERVES 1

2 slices thick bacon, cut into squares
2 tablespoons clarified butter, melted
3 extra-large eggs, beaten
2 to 3 tablespoons mozzarella, grated
3 cherry tomatoes, halved
1 lettuce leaf for decoration

Cook the bacon in a skillet, then remove and drain. Heat the butter in an omelet pan, and add the bacon. Sauté for about 1 minute. Add the beaten eggs and pull once with the fork. Add the cheese, pull again, then add the cherry tomatoes. Follow basic omelet-making directions. Serve this omelet on a lettuce leaf. Note that the butter will look darker in this recipe, but that won't affect the taste.

Rather than frying bacon—which always produces crinkly slices—we bake it to keep it flat. Our technique for sugar-backed bacon calls for laying strips of bacon on a cookie sheet and sprinkling the bacon with sugar to lightly coat just before popping the sheet in a 350-degree oven. In addition, the sugar caramelizes on the bacon, making the strips crispy and non-greasy. The bacon does not taste really sweet—just rich.

SOUR CREAM BLUEBERRY COFFEE CAKE

What better way to greet the morning than with a freshly baked coffee cake bursting with blueberries?

¾ cup sweet butter, softened
1 cup sugar
2 extra-large eggs
1 teaspoon vanilla extract
2 cups all-purpose flour
1 teaspoon baking powder
1 teaspoon baking soda
½ teaspoon salt
2½ cups blueberries

STREUSEL TOPPING

4 tablespoons sweet butter, melted
1 cup firmly packed brown sugar
2 teaspoons ground cinnamon
½ cup walnut pieces

Preheat oven to 350 degrees. Grease and flour a 10-inch tube pan.

Cream butter and sugar in large mixing bowl until light and fluffy. Add eggs, one at a time, beating well after each addition. Add the vanilla extract; beat very well.

Combine the flour, baking powder, baking soda, and salt in a separate bowl, then stir them into the butter mixture alternately with the sour cream, ending with the dry ingredients. Beat until very smooth. (This is a very dense batter, so do not be afraid to beat.) Fold in the blueberries.

FOR THE TOPPING:

Combine Streusel ingredients in a mixing bowl. Spread half the batter into prepared pan. Sprinkle with half of Streusel. Top with remaining batter, then remaining Streusel. Bake 50 to 55 minutes, until toothpick inserted in center comes out clean. Let cake cool in pan 10 minutes, then turn out onto wire rack to cool completely.

✿ ✿ ✿ ✿ ✿ ✿ ✿ ✿ ✿ ✿ ✿ ✿ ✿ ✿ ✿

We are very proud of our baked goods—the puffy biscuits, luscious cakes, and flaky fruit pies. These are our calling cards. We have spent many hours perfecting our recipes, and we are eager to pass along some of them to you. We always use all-purpose white flour without a leavening agent, and we use only large or extra-large eggs, depending on recipe requirements. Glass, porcelain, or stainless steel bowls work best for mixing. We urge you to know your oven so that you can depend on it! Regardless of what you are baking, always rotate pans in oven during the baking time, to ensure even browning.

✿ ✿ ✿ ✿ ✿ ✿ ✿ ✿ ✿ ✿ ✿ ✿ ✿ ✿

ANGEL BISCUITS

YIELDS
24

Our light, airy Angel Biscuits, a traditional Southern baked treat, contain three different kinds of leavening agents. In addition, we use shortening in them—the only baked goods we make with shortening—because it makes them "shorter" than butter does.

Follow every step carefully when you make these; they are worth the effort. When combining ingredients, be sure to add just the right amount of liquid to the dry: the texture should be spongy, not sticky.

2   tablespoons dried yeast
    pinch of sugar
¼   cup tepid water
5   cups all-purpose flour
2   tablespoons baking powder
¼   teaspoon baking soda
2   tablespoons sugar

½   teaspoon salt
1   cup vegetable shortening
1⅓ cups buttermilk, at room
    temperature
    flour for the biscuit cutter
    melted butter to brush tops

(continued on next page)

In a small bowl, dissolve the yeast with a pinch of the sugar in the tepid water. Preheat the oven to 350 degrees, and lightly grease a baking sheet.

Combine the flour, baking powder, baking soda, sugar and salt in a large mixing bowl. To prevent overhandling of the dough, use 2 knives to cut in the shortening until it resembles coarse meal. Add the yeast mixture. Then add the buttermilk and bring the dough together with your hands in a light kneading movement, making sure no dry ingredients have been left to settle to the bottom of the bowl. Like pie dough, this will have folds, so don't worry that it is not smooth. Turn the dough out onto a very lightly floured surface, and pat it out 1 to 1¼ inches thick. Dip a 2-inch biscuit cutter into flour before each cut. After cutting out the first biscuit, place it on the baking sheet. With the side of the biscuit cutter, push the dough together as you work, keeping it all in 1 piece. Handle as little as possible.

If you like soft biscuits, crowd them close together on the baking sheet so the sides don't become crusty; if you like crusty biscuits, bake them far apart. Either way, the insides remain tender. Bake for 18 to 20 minutes or until their tops turn golden; after baking, brush tops with melted butter.

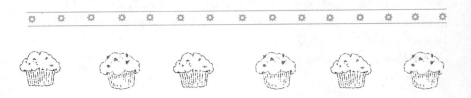

We think freshly baked muffins are a wonderful part of morning meals, and ours are so simple to make, you can have them ready for breakfast in almost no time at all. But it is imperative to follow several important steps for success. The butter should be neither too warm nor too cold; it must be just soft enough to mush in your hand. Beat it with the sugar. Thoroughly combine all the dry ingredients so that the leavening agent is well distributed throughout. Mix together all the liquid ingredients, then make a well in the center of the dry ingredients, and add the liquid quickly. Do not overstir, barely incorporating dry ingredients: you want the batter to be lumpy or the muffins will be dry. Never let the batter sit because the leavening agents react quickly to the liquid, so bake the muffins immediately. Instead of using butter, which adds more fat to the recipe, we line our tins with paper liners so the muffins never stick. Our muffins are large, and they rise and puff out over the sides of the muffin tin during baking, so don't be alarmed when they do!

✿ ✿ ✿ ✿ ✿ ✿ ✿ ✿ ✿ ✿ ✿ ✿ ✿ ✿ ✿

BLUEBERRY MUFFINS

YIELDS 12

These amply portioned blueberry muffins recapture yet another childhood memory of ours—muffins baked fresh daily at the Jordan Marsh Department Store, Boston. We waited in line to buy them hot, wrapped in wax paper, and ate them walking along the streets, savoring the juicy berries and cakey muffins. What makes these unique is their crunchy top.

    8 tablespoons sweet butter, softened
   ¾ cup sugar
    1 extra-large egg
    1 teaspoon vanilla extract
    1 cup milk
  2½ cups all-purpose flour
   ½ teaspoon salt
    1 tablespoon baking powder
 1½ cups fresh or frozen blueberries
    1 tablespoon sugar, plus 1 teaspoon cinnamon,
      mixed for topping

(continued on next page)

Preheat the oven to 350 degrees. Line the muffin tins with paper liners.

Cream the butter and sugar together in a mixing bowl until thoroughly mixed but still lumpy. Add the egg and vanilla, beating until smooth with a wooden spoon. Gradually add the milk, stirring well to combine.

In a separate bowl, sift together the flour, salt and baking powder, then fold the wet ingredients into the dry, stirring just enough to incorporate. With a metal spoon, stir in the blueberries in a figure 8 motion—this prevents the berries from breaking open and bleeding. Divide the batter among 12 lined muffin tins, filling each to the top. Sprinkle each with a portion of the sugar. Bake 20 to 25 minutes.

ORANGE BRAN MUFFINS

YIELDS
8

½ cup sweet butter, softened
¼ cup brown sugar
½ cup dark molasses
 1 extra-large egg
½ cup orange juice
½ cup sour cream
 1 cup all-purpose flour
 1 cup bran
 1 teaspoon baking soda
   grated zest of 1 orange
½ cup golden raisins

Preheat oven to 350 degrees. Line the muffin tins with paper liners.

Cream the butter and sugar in a large mixing bowl, then add the molasses, egg, orange juice and sour cream. Combine the flour, bran and baking soda in a separate bowl. Fold the dry ingredients into the wet, then stir in the orange zest and the raisins. Fill muffin tins. Bake for 20 to 25 minutes.

BANANA MUFFINS

YIELDS
7

6 tablespoons sweet butter, melted
½ cup maple syrup
1 large egg
1 teaspoon vanilla
2 ripe medium-sized bananas
1½ cups flour
½ teaspoon salt
1 teaspoon baking powder
1 teaspoon baking soda
½ cup walnut pieces

Preheat the oven to 400 degrees. Line muffin tins with paper liners.

Combine the butter, maple syrup, egg and vanilla in a mixing bowl. In a separate bowl, mash bananas well with a fork, then add them to the butter-egg mixture.

Combine the flour, salt, baking powder and baking soda in another mixing bowl, stirring well. Then add the walnut pieces, reserving 1 tablespoon for topping the muffins. Add the liquid to the dry ingredients, and mix just until moist. Fill the muffin tins ⅔ full, and sprinkle remaining walnuts over top. Bake for 20 to 25 minutes.

✿   ✿   ✿   ✿   ✿   ✿   ✿   ✿   ✿   ✿   ✿   ✿   ✿   ✿

Some of the most impressive garnishes and condiments are the simplest to make. Fruit butters make a delicious spread for almost all baked goods and pastries. You can make them quickly by whipping softened sweet butter with a fruit jam or jelly of your choice. The proportions are 1 pound of butter to ½ cup thick fruit mixture. Serve the butter to family and friends and delight them!

✿   ✿   ✿   ✿   ✿   ✿   ✿   ✿   ✿   ✿   ✿   ✿   ✿   ✿   ✿

APPLE SPICE MUFFINS

¼ cup sweet butter, softened
½ cup firmly packed brown sugar
1 teaspoon ground cinnamon
¼ teaspoon ground allspice
1 extra-large egg
2 cups all-purpose flour
2 teaspoons baking powder
½ teaspoon baking soda
¾ cup milk
½ cup chopped apple

TOPPING

2 tablespoons sweet butter
¼ cup brown sugar

Preheat oven to 350 degrees. Line the muffin tins with paper liners.

Cream butter and sugar in mixing bowl. Stir in the spices and the egg. Combine the flour, baking powder and baking soda in a separate bowl; add them to the butter mixture alternately with the milk, stirring just to combine.

To make the topping, melt the 2 tablespoons of butter and combine with the ¼ cup of sugar.

Fill muffin tins ⅔ full with batter. Top each with a portion of the topping mixture. Bake 20 to 25 minutes.

STICKY BUNS

A hot, cinnamony sticky bun, served with jam and butter, is delicious for breakfast or dessert.

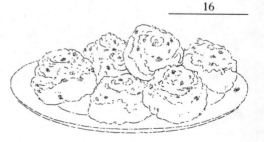

2 packages dry yeast
  pinch plus 2 tablespoons sugar
¼ cup warm water
4 cups all-purpose flour
½ teaspoon salt
1 cup warm milk
2 tablespoons sweet butter, melted

FILLING

6 tablespoons sweet butter, melted
½ cup cinnamon sugar
½ cup sugar
¾ cup raisins
3½ cups pecan pieces combined with
  1 tablespoon ground cinnamon

SYRUP

3 tablespoons sweet
  butter, melted
¾ cup honey
2½ cups firmly packed
  brown sugar

Some bakers swear that they can taste the difference between fresh and dried baking yeast. We use fresh in the restaurant but don't feel there is much of a difference. Using fresh yeast can be tricky if you are not absolutely certain it is fresh; dried is foolproof if you use it before its package expiration date.

Lightly grease large bowl. Set aside. Grease 16-by-11-inch pan.

In a small bowl, sprinkle yeast and a pinch of sugar over the water; stir, and set aside to proof. (See the glossary for instructions on how to proof.) Combine the flour, the 2 tablespoons sugar and the salt in a separate large bowl. Stir in milk and butter; stir in yeast mixture until well blended. Turn dough out onto lightly floured surface and knead 10 to 12 minutes, until smooth and elastic. Place dough in greased bowl, turning to coat entire surface. Cover and let rise in a warm place until double in volume.

Meanwhile, for filling, combine butter, cinnamon sugar and sugar. Set aside. For syrup, combine the butter, honey and sugar. Set aside. When dough has risen, punch down and, on lightly floured surface, roll out into a 12-by-18-inch rectangle. Visually divide dough into 3 equal sections: A, B and C. Fold C over B and A over C. Give dough a ¼ turn, and again roll out into a 12-by-18-inch rectangle. Again give a ¼ turn and repeat folding, then refrigerate dough for 20 minutes.

Roll out dough on lightly floured surface, and repeat folding and turning procedure twice more. Roll out into a 12-by-18-inch rectangle. Add raisins and ½ cup of the pecans to the filling and spread evenly over the dough. Roll up jelly-roll fashion and cut into 1-inch-thick slices. Pour syrup into a 16-by-11-inch baking pan; sprinkle with remaining pecans. Place rolls cut side down on top of pecans. Cover, and let rise until almost doubled.

Preheat oven to 375 degrees. Bake buns 25 to 30 minutes, until golden. Line another baking sheet with aluminum foil; lightly grease foil. Turn buns out onto greased foil. Let cool 10 minutes. Pull apart and eat!

HASH BROWNS

A morning meal wouldn't be complete without a generous serving of potatoes, and we have concocted 2 potato recipes, both so good you may want to prepare them for lunch and dinner as well. The first is our simple version of hash browns, calling for cooked new potatoes combined with vegetables and seasonings. For a heartier meal, add bacon or sausage, and melted cheese.

 ½ cup sweet butter
 1 onion, diced
 2 red bell peppers, diced
 2 green bell peppers, diced
 1 teaspoon kosher salt
 1 teaspoon ground white pepper
 1 tablespoon paprika
 ¼ teaspoon chili powder
 ½ teaspoon dried thyme, crushed
 3 pounds unpeeled new potatoes,
   parboiled, drained and quartered

Preheat oven to 450 degrees. Melt the butter in a heavy skillet over medium heat, then place the onion, bell peppers and spices in the skillet and cook until onion and peppers are softened. Add potatoes, raise heat slightly, then flatten all ingredients with a spatula. Once the bottoms of the vegetables have browned, turn them over, flattening them again. Brown the other side. When cooked, place the skillet in the oven for 15 minutes to give the potatoes a crunchy crust. Serve immediately.

OUR SPECIAL BREAKFAST POTATOES

SHOULD
SERVE AT
LEAST 2
PEOPLE

Ann's father provided us with the basis for our second recipe. It is extraordinarily good, but you must watch over the ingredients while they cook. This pancakelike dish must be very thin and very crisp.

    8 tablespoons clarified butter
    4 tablespoons chopped onion
    2 Idaho potatoes, grated
    ½ teaspoon kosher salt
       dash of pepper

Heat butter in skillet over high heat until butter just begins to smoke. Add the onion and cook 1 minute, stirring occasionally. Add the potatoes, distributing them evenly over the pan; do not flatten. Add salt and pepper. When the edges start to curl and brown, flip the entire pancake with a spatula. Turn heat to medium and sauté until the pancake is golden on both sides, about 8 minutes.

Keep potatoes warm, uncovered, in 200-degree oven while making additional servings, if needed.

2

LUNCHTIME

Poor lunch. We think it's the most neglected, glossed-over meal of the day, an orphan sandwiched in between meetings, chores and appointments. Unless people actually turn it into a two-drink affair, they are most likely to skip lunch altogether, or grab a street vendor's snack, or pause with a friend for an unexciting bowl of salad.

We believe lunch should be a cheerful midday break, structured to put people into a good mood. It should also be substantial enough to energize them to finish up the day's work. In our sunny restaurants, we aim to give customers a reason to enjoy this noontime meal on its own merits —not just as a business meeting or a hunger-quelling necessity. We believe that even the busiest executive should take time out

for a leisurely noon meal break. And all customers—playwright, housewife, lawyer and accountant—should feel enough at home to read a novel, sort through mail, talk to friends or eat in comfortable silence. Most of our lunches can be portable, should a customer prefer a sunny park bench or quiet conference room. Our lunches, with their heft and unusual combinations, are really a holdover from European childhood traditions, when Mother packed up a lunch pail with a container of soup or stew, fresh bread and fruit, and imaginative sandwiches that today's child (and adult) would envy.

These meals at Good Enough to Eat often incorporate leftovers from the night before—roasts sliced up, then sandwiched between slices of crusty bread, chilled vegetables tossed together for a nutritious salad, and everywhere we can, foods sparked with ketchup, mustard and other tempting condiments.

Soups

Few foods we know evoke such a sense of well-being and comfort as made-from-scratch soups simmering on the back burner. Although soups appear on our dinner menu, they hold center stage at lunch, winter and summer, and come to table steaming or iced in big bowls. Our robust soups, thickly textured with meats, vegetables and legumes, could satisfy the hungriest ranch hand. When served—in generous portions, of course—with fresh bread, they become a meal in themselves.

Our cooks would agree that soup making is a thoroughly creative outlet, and one they look forward to. Delicious soups can be concocted from any number of ingredients—even leftovers. The trick for the soup maker is to be as ingenious and flexible as good sense allows. If a recipe calls for sausage, and all that's on hand is frankfurters, then feel free to substitute. As with any meal, however, put together compatible ingredients and don't go overboard with seasonings. And best of all, soups are so independent that they can simmer quietly without the constant care other dishes require.

Our soups always begin with homemade stock. We then add fresh and/or leftover ingredients. In general, we find that canned stocks are too salty. We cut up our fresh vegetables carefully, because their shape does determine cooking time—the only aspect of soup making that demands special attention. We don't want to overcook vegetables, because they should retain their crunch. We fry our spices before adding them to soups, sweat onions and celery to extract maximum flavor, and we quickly fry vegetables in the stockpot before adding liquid.

Learning to cut onions the professional way is, in our opinion, the most important knife skill to master. It's also quick, easy once learned, and results in relatively few tears. Cut off the pointy side of the onion. Halve the onion through the root and peel it. Place the cut side down on the cutting surface with the root to the left. Next, make lengthwise slices at ⅛-inch intervals by inserting the tip of the knife near, but not through, the root and slicing down toward the pointy end, following the curve of the onion. Each slice should angle toward the center of the onion.

Then, cut three slices parallel to the cutting surface, going toward, but not through, the root.

Next, place your fingers on top of the onion, knuckles facing right, fingers slightly curled in with the blade resting along your knuckles to guide it. Slice the onion crosswise with a rocking movement, each slice coming closer to the root. This will give you small squares of onion.

Homemade stocks may be time-consuming, but they provide the tastiest base for soups and stews, as well as for
sauces and gravies. We've given some tips on stock making with the hopes that you will take the time to make
your stocks, and enhance your meals. Wise cooks save
all vegetable parings and trimmings, except parsley
greens and garlic skins, for stock making. (Color drains
quickly from parsley greens and both items spoil easily.)
Wrap everything in plastic bags and store in the refrigerator until you are ready to make the stock.

For a successful vegetable stock, follow these instructions: In a large pot, place 2 onions cut in half, and any
other onion peels you have saved, 1/2 head garlic peeled
and mashed to extract the flavor, 2 or 3 carrots and any
peelings, celery tops or 5 or 6 celery stalks cut up, the
stem ends of 2 parsley bunches, 2 leeks cleaned and
chopped, any mushroom bottoms (if you have some), 1
hot red chili (if desired), 2 teaspoons salt and 2 cloves.
Add 1/4 cup vegetable oil. Place the pot over medium
heat for 10 minutes. Then add water to cover ingredients, and bring to a boil. Reduce the heat, stirring occasionally to remove any scum from the surface. Add 3 bay
leaves, 6 peppercorns (if you omitted the hot chili), 2
teaspoons basil, 2 teaspoons thyme, 2 teaspoons sage,
and 2 teaspoons rosemary. Do not cook more than 2
hours—after that time, the vegetables apparently reab-
sorb their flavors.

To make chicken stock, use 2 whole chickens cut up, or the equivalent in parts. Fill a large stockpot with cold water, and add salt, 12 peppercorns, and the chicken. Bring to a boil, skim the scum off the surface, then lower the heat to a simmer. Add 3 peeled onions (each stuck with 1 whole clove), 2 dried hot red chilies, and a handful of dried, or preferably fresh, herbs including thyme, rosemary, sage and 4 bay leaves. Also add 6 garlic cloves, cut-up celery stalks, carrots and the stem ends of two parsley bunches. Simmer all this for about 2 hours, and your stock will be ready.

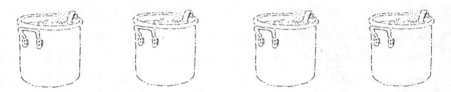

To make beef stock, use 15 to 20 pounds beef bones. Lay them in a roasting pan. Add 4 onions, 4 peeled carrots and 6 clean celery stalks. Sprinkle salt and pepper over to taste, and a few tablespoons of vegetable oil. Roast everything for 3 to 4 hours. Then remove from the roasting pan, and place all ingredients in a large stockpot with water to cover. Deglaze the roasting pan and save the remaining juice, if you like. Add 4 bay leaves, a pinch of dried herbs, 12 peppercorns and the stem ends of 2 bunches of parsley. Bring to a boil and skim off the surface, then reduce heat and simmer, skimming regularly. Cook for 4 to 6 hours.

VEGETABLE CHOWDER

SERVES
8

*D*espite its French origins, this chowder is an all-American dish because of the added corn.

   3 cups chopped celery (about 1 bunch)
1½ onions, chopped
   ¾ teaspoon minced garlic
   ¾ teaspoon kosher salt
   ½ teaspoon black pepper
   ¼ cup olive oil
   4 cups vegetable stock
1¾ cups quartered unpeeled new potatoes or
      peeled cubed sweet potatoes
   ¼ cup white wine
   1 bay leaf
   ¼ teaspoon cumin
   6 sprigs fresh thyme, or 2 teaspoons dried
   2 cups broccoli florets
   3 cups carrot circles
   4 cups corn kernels
   2 cups heavy cream

In stockpot, sweat (see glossary) celery, onions and garlic with salt and pepper in oil over low heat for 15 minutes. Add stock, potatoes and wine. Bring to a boil and reduce the heat to medium. Add 2 cups water, the bay leaf, cumin and thyme. Cook 40 minutes. Add broccoli, carrots and corn; cook 5 minutes longer. Add a ladleful of hot soup to the cream, then return the mixture to stockpot, stirring. Do not boil once the cream is in.

CHICKEN NOODLE SOUP

SERVES
8

*L*ike Mom's or Grandma's, this really homey soup must be made from scratch. Its flavor comes from homemade stock.

  2 large onions, chopped
  6 stalks celery, chopped
  5 tablespoons vegetable oil
  1 pound carrots, chunked
  1 pound uncooked chicken breast cut into 1-inch strips or cooked meat of 2 pounds chicken
10 cups homemade chicken stock
  1 teaspoon salt
  1 teaspoon ground white pepper
  1 bay leaf
  1 teaspoon chopped fresh thyme
  1 cup sliced mushrooms
  1 cup uncooked egg noodles or rice
 ¼ cup chopped fresh parsley

thyme

Sweat onions and celery in oil in stockpot over low heat for 15 minutes, until soft. Add carrots, stock, salt, pepper, bay leaf and thyme, and simmer 30 to 35 minutes. Add mushrooms, pasta or rice, and parsley, and simmer 20 minutes longer. Add chicken 10 minutes before finishing. Correct seasonings.

CABBAGE BEEF SOUP

SERVES
8 TO 10

*A*ccompany a bowl of this soup with coarse black bread and cheese, perhaps some wine, and enjoy a feast.

 4 pounds stewing beef or flanken
 ½ cup vegetable oil
 ½ cup red wine
 6 stalks celery, chopped
 2 onions, chopped
 2 cloves garlic, minced
 3 cups canned plum tomatoes, crushed into small pieces

3 cups canned crushed tomatoes
¾ cup firmly packed brown sugar
¼ cup lemon juice
6 cups beef stock
2 tablespoons kosher salt
1 teaspoon ground pepper
2 teaspoons chopped fresh thyme or 1 teaspoon dried
1 bay leaf
1 green cabbage (about 1 pound) shredded

Brown meat in ¼ cup vegetable oil. Pour off all but 1 tablespoon oil. Deglaze the pot with wine and reduce the liquid by half. Add 1 cup water, cover, and simmer for 1 to 1½ hours.

Meanwhile, sweat celery, onions and garlic in ¼ cup oil. Cook until soft, about 15 to 20 minutes. Add tomatoes, sugar, lemon juice, stock, salt, pepper, thyme and bay leaf. Cook 1 hour. Add drained meat and cabbage; cook over medium heat 1 hour longer. Correct seasoning.

SPLIT PEA SOUP

SERVES
8 TO 10

*I*n cafés in Holland, big bowls of pea soup served with dark bread for mopping up the bowl are complete meals. Serve this soup with a stein of dark beer.

1 large onion, chopped
4 stalks celery, chopped
2 cloves garlic, minced
2 tablespoons butter
2 tablespoons vegetable oil
1 ham hock or leftover ham bone
1 pound dried split peas, washed and drained
7 cups beef stock
1 tablespoon brown sugar
2 teaspoons kosher salt
1 teaspoon ground black pepper
1 bay leaf
1 pound carrots, chunked
1 tablespoon chopped fresh thyme, or 1 teaspoon dried

(continued on next page)

Sweat onion, celery, and garlic in butter and oil 15 to 20 minutes, until soft. Add ham hock or bone, peas, stock, sugar, salt, pepper and bay leaf. Cook over medium heat 1 hour. Add carrots and thyme and cook 45 minutes longer. Check for seasonings.

LENTIL SOUP

*L*entils are commonly associated with Indian cuisine, but nourishing lentil soup is also an Eastern European staple.

- 6 stalks celery, chopped
- 2 onions, chopped
- 4 cloves garlic, minced
- 2 teaspoons kosher salt
- 1 teaspoon pepper
- 1 teaspoon curry powder
- 1 teaspoon cumin
- ½ cup vegetable oil
- ½ cup sherry
- 3 cups water
- 3 cups beef stock, homemade
- 2 cups dried lentils, cleaned
- 2 cups drained canned plum tomatoes
- 2 tablespoons ketchup
- 1 teaspoon brown sugar
- 1 teaspoon chopped fresh thyme or ½ teaspoon dried
- 2 bay leaves
- 2 pounds carrots, sliced in ¼-inch circles

Sweat celery, onions, garlic, salt, pepper, curry powder and cumin in oil over low heat 15 to 20 minutes, or until soft. Raise heat, add sherry, and reduce the liquid to 2 tablespoons. Add 3 cups water and remaining ingredients except carrots. Bring to a boil, then reduce heat and simmer 1 hour. Add carrots and simmer 30 minutes longer, or until lentils and carrots are cooked. Correct seasoning.

MUSHROOM-BARLEY SOUP

*T*he British and Scots love barley, as well they should, for this nutritious grain tastes delicious in stews, baked on its own, or made into a thick soup like this one.

- 4 stalks celery, chopped
- 1 large onion, chopped
- 2 cloves garlic, minced
- 2 teaspoons kosher salt
- 1 teaspoon pepper
- ½ cup vegetable oil
- 9 cups beef stock
- 1 pound pearl barley
- 1 bay leaf
- ½ teaspoon chopped fresh thyme or 1 teaspoon dried thyme
- 4 cups sliced mushrooms
- 2 egg yolks
- 1 cup heavy cream
- 4 tablespoons chopped fresh parsley

Sweat celery, onion, garlic, salt and pepper in oil in stockpot over low heat 15 to 20 minutes, or until soft. Add stock, barley, bay leaf and thyme. Stir well, bring to a boil, and simmer for 1 hour. Add mushrooms, and cook 30 minutes longer, or until barley is soft.

Make the *liaison* (see glossary) by whisking yolks with the cream in small bowl. Add a ladleful of hot soup to the egg mixture, stirring constantly so the eggs do not curdle, then return to soup, whisking in slowly. Cook over low heat 10 minutes longer. Do not let soup boil after this addition. Garnish each bowl with parsley to serve.

Vegetarian Dishes

Many of our customers are vegetarians, so we always offer at least 1 all-vegetable entree at lunchtime. Vegetarian food can lack culinary character, but we feel ours is distinctive. Carrie was a vegetarian herself for 4 years, and quickly learned the knack of creating exciting, colorful, tempting vegetarian dishes.

She invented our offerings of stuffed vegetables. Our stuffed vegetables look for all the world like Walt Disney cartoon characters from *Fantasia*. Since the stuffing fits into the vegetable itself, the vegetables' beautiful natural colors and shapes require no extra garnishes. These are full lunches (dinners too) and not side dishes. Yet, these leftovers can make perfect accompaniments to a meat-based dinner for nonvegetarians. You will need a mortar and pestle for the recipe below.

Our other vegetarian entrees are so rich and satisfying that they, too, are complete meals.

Garlic adds tremendous flavor to meals, so you must be sure to use proper quantities to achieve the desired taste. Here are our suggestions for preparing it: Select garlic heads that are firm, not soft or with flaky skin. Peel cloves off the head with a forceful whack by the palm of your hand, or the flat blade of a knife, to loosen them. Again with a flat blade, smash each clove without disconnecting it from the others. This loosens the skin so it peels off the clove easily. Pare off the root end and any bruises. Follow the same cutting steps as for chopping onions (see p. 46), rocking the knife blade back and forth until garlic is finely minced. With the exception of roasted garlic, which is common in Provençal cooking, garlic has such a strong taste that, if the pieces are not tiny, they impart an unpleasant taste to other ingredients being cooked with them.

STUFFED VEGETABLES

STUFFED ZUCCHINI

- 2 tablespoons sweet butter, melted
- ¼ pound fresh spinach, cleaned and chopped
- 2 cloves garlic, minced
- ½ teaspoon kosher salt
- ¼ teaspoon ground pepper
- ¼ teaspoon paprika
- 4 large zucchini
- ¼ cup olive oil
- 1 cup sour cream
- 1 cup grated Cheddar cheese
- ⅓ cup roasted walnuts

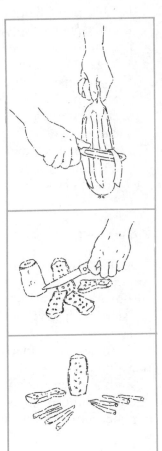

STUFFED TOMATOES

- 8 beefsteak tomatoes
- 1 teaspoon minced garlic
- 1 onion, halved and thinly sliced
- 2 tablespoons olive oil
- 1 teaspoon kosher salt
- 1 teaspoon ground pepper
- 1 bunch broccoli, florets only
- 3 zucchini, halved and cut in ¼-inch-thick slices
- ½ pound mushrooms, chopped
- ½ cup red wine
- 1 tablespoon tomato paste
- 1 teaspoon dried basil
- 1 teaspoon dried thyme

STUFFED PEPPERS

  8 medium or 4 large green bell peppers
  1 tablespoon chopped fresh sage, or 1 teaspoon powdered dried
  1 tablespoon chopped fresh oregano, or 1½ teaspoons dried
  1 tablespoon chopped fresh basil, or 1½ teaspoons dried
  1 tablespoon chopped fresh parsley
  3 large cloves garlic, minced
  4 cups cooked white rice
  3 tablespoons drained capers
  ½ cup grated Parmesan cheese
  ½ cup olive oil
  2 tablespoons lemon juice
  ½ teaspoon ground pepper
16 pitted black olives, julienned

Preheat oven to 325 degrees.

TO MAKE THE ZUCCHINI: In butter, sauté the spinach with the garlic, salt, pepper, paprika and mustard over low heat to make a chiffonade. Cut ends from zucchini, halve lengthwise, and drizzle cut sides with olive oil. Bake 5 to 10 minutes so they lose their raw look.

Combine the spinach with the sour cream, half the cheese, and the walnuts.

With a spoon, scoop the seeds from the zucchini. Fill each with equal amount of spinach mixture, then top with remaining Cheddar cheese. Place on baking sheet with the peppers.

TO MAKE THE TOMATOES: Cut tops from tomatoes, and with a spoon carve out seeds and center core without tearing the sides and bottoms of the tomatoes. Bake cut side down 6 to 10 minutes, until slightly soft.

Sauté garlic and onion in oil with salt and pepper over low heat for 5 minutes. Add broccoli, zucchini and mushrooms and cook, stirring, 3 minutes longer. Add wine, tomato paste, basil and thyme, and reduce the liquid to almost nothing. Cool slightly and fill tomatoes equally with mixture. Place tomatoes on baking sheet with stuffed peppers and zucchini. Bake all for 15 minutes, or until hot. Serve 1 of each vegetable to each person.

TO MAKE THE PEPPERS: If using medium peppers, cut off the tops and save. If using large peppers, halve them. Remove membrane and seeds. Cut a slice from the bottom if necessary to make them stand. Bake 10 to 15 minutes on a cookie sheet, until soft but not totally cooked. Set aside.

Chop sage and oregano plus basil and parsley. Place in a pestle with the garlic and grind into a paste.

In a separate bowl, combine the rice, capers, cheese, olive oil, lemon juice and pepper. Add the ground herbs and the olives. Mix well and fill the peppers. Put the tops back on the peppers if you like the look. Place on baking sheet.

VEGETARIAN CHILI

SERVES
4 TO 6

- 1 tablespoon kosher salt
- ¾ teaspoon black pepper
- 1 tablespoon chili powder
- 2 teaspoons paprika
- 1 teaspoon dry mustard
- ¼ to ½ teaspoon cayenne
- 1 tablespoon dried cumin
- 1 tablespoon anise seeds
- ⅓ cup clarified butter
- 1 large onion, sliced
- 5 medium cloves garlic, chopped
- 2 stalks celery, chopped
- 1 large eggplant, degorged (see glossary) and cut into 1-inch cubes
- 2 small yellow squash, carefully peeled so outside is still yellow, cored and cubed
- 1 red bell pepper, julienned
- 1 green bell pepper, julienned
- 4 plum tomatoes
- ½ cup olive oil
- 14-ounce can plum tomatoes, crushed into small pieces
- 2 teaspoons chopped fresh thyme
- 1 teaspoon dried rosemary
- 2 teaspoons dried basil

(continued on next page)

1 bay leaf
1 teaspoon Worcestershire sauce
  grated rind of half an orange or lemon
2 tablespoons honey
1 tablespoon ketchup
2 to 3 zucchini, striped with peeler, and cut into ½-inch-thick
  circles
    11- to 13-ounce can black beans, drained
    11- to 13-ounce can kidney beans, drained
    11- to 13-ounce can black-eyed peas, drained
¼ bunch fresh parsley, chopped
2 cups cooked brown rice

TOPPINGS

1 cup sour cream
1 red onion, chopped
¼ pound sharp Cheddar cheese, grated

A quick note on cayenne: Purchase a good quality, otherwise it will have stale taste and lack punch.

Fry the salt, pepper, chili powder, paprika, mustard, cayenne, cumin and anise seeds in butter for 5 to 6 minutes. Add onion, garlic and celery and cook over medium heat 5 to 10 minutes until vegetables are soft. Add all remaining ingredients except zucchini, beans, peas, parsley and rice. Simmer, stirring often, for 25 minutes. Add zucchini, beans and peas; cook 10 minutes longer. Stir in parsley. Correct seasonings (if more spices are needed, remember to fry them first).

Serve chili in bowls over brown rice, with bowls of toppings (above) on the side to add as desired.

VEGETARIAN LASAGNA

SERVES
8 TO 10

1 large red bell pepper, julienned
1 large green bell pepper, julienned
1 bunch broccoli, cut into florets
1 small head cauliflower, cut into florets
1 pound carrots, peeled and cut into ¼-inch circles
1 pound zucchini, striped and cut into ⅛-inch circles
1 pound mushrooms thinly sliced

CHEESE MIX

3 pounds ricotta cheese
½ to 1 cup heavy cream (optional)
½ pound mozzarella cheese, cut into small cubes
½ pound Gruyère cheese, cubed very small
5 cloves garlic, minced
1½ teaspoons kosher salt
1½ teaspoons white pepper
½ teaspoon paprika
½ teaspoon dry mustard
2 teaspoons dried basil
2 teaspoons dried oregano
½ cup olive oil
2 eggs
9 to 10 cups Meatless Tomato Sauce (recipe on page 60), at room temperature
1 pound lasagne noodles (15 to 17 strips) cooked *al dente*, strips separated
½ pound mozzarella cheese, thinly sliced
½ pound Parmesan cheese, freshly grated

Bring 4 quarters water to a boil, and blanch all vegetables except zucchini and mushrooms for 1½ minutes after water returns to a boil. Remove vegetables and shock them under cold running water. Combine cooked and raw vegetables.

Preheat oven to 350 degrees.

Combine ingredients for Cheese Mix, using cream, if necessary, to bring ricotta to a soft ice-creamlike consistency.

Spread 1 cup tomato sauce in pan. Lay down ⅓ of the pasta.

Spread half the cheese mixture over pasta. Add half of the combined vegetables. Cover with 3 cups tomato sauce, and ⅓ of the pasta. Repeat with remaining cheese mixture, vegetables, the rest of the pasta, and 2½ cups tomato sauce. Top with sliced mozzarella, then with grated Parmesan cheese.

Place baking pan on cookie sheet and bake 45 minutes, until heated all the way through. If the lasagna is getting too dark, but is still not heated through and bubbling on sides, cover with foil to finish the baking.

Serve with garlic bread and a nice green salad.

If you will not be using this quantity all at once, bake in 2 pans for 25 to 30 minutes; when second pan is completely cool, wrap lasagna for the freezer.   •

MEATLESS TOMATO SAUCE

YIELDS 5½ TO 6 QUARTS

½ cup olive oil
3 large onions (2 pounds), finely chopped
4 to 6 cloves garlic, minced
1 small carrot, peeled and cut into thin strips
1 tablespoon kosher salt
2 teaspoons white pepper
2 cups red wine
9 six-ounce cans crushed tomatoes
9 six-ounce cans stewed plum tomatoes, crushed with your hand
3 pounds fresh plum tomatoes, diced
2 tablespoons tomato paste
2 teaspoons dried basil
2 teaspoons dried oregano
1 teaspoon dried marjoram (optional)
1 teaspoon dried thyme
3 bay leaves

oregano

Sweat (see glossary) carrot, onions, garlic, salt and pepper in the oil over medium heat, stirring often. Add wine, stirring up brown bits from bottom of pot, and reduce wine to ½ to 1 cup. Add remaining ingredients. Bring almost to a boil, stir, and reduce heat. Simmer at least 2 hours, stirring often, keeping covered during the second hour.

MACARONI AND CHEESE

SERVES
6 TO 8

  2 pounds ziti
  6 cups White Sauce (recipe follows)
  ½ pound smoked mozzarella, grated
  ½ pound plain mozzarella, grated
  ½ pound white Cheddar cheese, grated
  ½ pound cooked ham or cooked bacon
  3 tablespoons grated Parmesan cheese
  3 tablespoons bread crumbs
  4 tablespoons sweet butter, softened

Cook ziti *al dente* according to package instructions. Meanwhile, preheat oven to 350 degrees. Grease an 18- by-12-inch ovenproof dish.

Make white sauce; cool slightly and add grated mozzarellas and Cheddar cheese. Add sauce and ham or bacon to ziti and mix well. Place in prepared baking dish, top with Parmesan and bread crumbs, and dot with butter. Bake 40 minutes.

WHITE SAUCE

MAKES
7 CUPS

  7 cups milk
  2 bay leaves
  1 bunch parsley stems
     sprig of thyme (optional)
  3 white peppercorns
  3 cups sweet butter
1½ teaspoons kosher salt

  1 teaspoon ground
     white pepper
  ¼ teaspoon paprika
  ¼ teaspoon dry mustard
1½ cups all-purpose flour
  ½ cup white wine

Combine milk with bay leaves, parsley stems, thyme, if using, and peppercorns. Scald milk; do not boil. Simmer gently 5 to 10 minutes, until well blended.

Meanwhile, combine butter, salt, pepper, paprika and mustard in a separate saucepan over low heat. Melt butter, but be careful not to burn. Stir in flour and cook, stirring constantly, 5 to 7 minutes. Add the wine and combine well. Strain milk and whisk in. Cook, stirring, 4 to 5 minutes; the sauce will thicken up suddenly. If not using the sauce immediately, drizzle some melted butter on top. Spread butter over surface with a damp paper towel so a skin will not form.

◇◇◇

We always recommend using fresh herbs whenever possible for their intense flavor, which accents and glorifies food. The only times we use dried herbs are when fresh seasonal herbs are not in the market, or when we want to flavor a slow-cooking dish, like a stew or soup, where the fresh herbs might turn an unpleasant color. To get full flavor from dried herbs, rub them between your thumb and forefinger before using. Never fry herbs; add them only to liquid once it is in the pot.

◇◇◇

Salads

Without doubt, fanciful salads are this decade's fastest-growing food sensation. Salad bars are sprouting up all across the country, and obviously many health-conscious Americans have accepted that an overflowing bowl of salad—not just greens alone—provides a wholesome alternative to the standard hot-plate luncheon entree.

Our bountiful salads, delicious main-event meals, often contain some striking taste and texture combinations. For us, a salad is a perfect place for leftovers, yet we strive for a combination of pure tastes. We don't cheat or mask anything under gloppy dressings. In a way, salads are difficult to make, because we must find light ingredients that mound well. We generally dress our salads with either our Vinaigrette or Mayonnaise (recipes follow).

VINAIGRETTE

YIELDS
3 CUPS

⅔ cup Dijon mustard
1 teaspoon kosher salt
1 teaspoon white pepper
1 teaspoon sweet paprika
⅓ cup fresh lemon juice
⅓ cup red wine vinegar
2⅔ to 3 cups olive oil and vegetable oil combined
　　in proportions to individual taste
　(All ingredients must be at room temperature)

Place bowl on damp towel to hold it securely.

Whisk mustard with salt, pepper and paprika. Drizzle in lemon juice, then vinegar, whisking constantly. Make sure all the mustard is incorporated. Scrape sides with a rubber spatula. Slowly drizzle in the oils in the center of the bowl, whisking nonstop until all the oil is emulsified. Taste for seasoning.

If vinaigrette curdles, add some mustard in another bowl, then whisk the vinaigrette into that.

We are salt people and use it liberally in our cooking. In the interest of health, we use kosher salt in our recipes calling for salt; it has a more intense flavor than regular table salt so less is required.

We personally dislike the strong, heavy taste of extra-virgin olive oil. It can overpower delicate ingredients and in salads it's so heavy it sinks to the bottom of the bowl. We use odorless pure olive oil instead. (Carrie hates the smell of olive oil. When in college in Aix-en-Provence, she lived next door to an olive oil factory.)

Our advice on paprika: get the freshest and best. We recommend Hungarian sweet paprika.

MAYONNAISE

YIELDS
4½ TO 5
CUPS

- 3 egg yolks
- 2 teaspoons kosher salt
- 2 teaspoons white pepper
- ¼ teaspoon paprika
- 1 tablespoon Dijon mustard
- ¼ cup fresh lemon juice
- 4 cups olive oil

Place bowl on a damp towel so it will not move around. Place yolks in blender bowl of food processor, add salt, pepper, paprika and mustard, and whisk, scraping down sides of bowl, until well blended. Drizzle with lemon juice, then gradually drizzle in the oil a drop at a time, completely incorporating it before adding more. Mayonnaise should be emulsified by the time the last third of the oil is being added.

VEGETABLE SALAD

SERVES
6

O ne of our most popular summer dishes is composed of a variety of fresh vegetables, tossed with grated cheese and vinaigrette and served on a bed of three different lettuces.

     1   small head of Romaine lettuce, rinsed and trimmed
     1   small head of Boston lettuce, rinsed and trimmed
     1   small head of red-leaf lettuce, rinsed and trimmed
     1   bunch watercress, rinsed and trimmed
     3   carrots, peeled and julienned
    10   mushrooms, cleaned and sliced
     1   red pepper, julienned
     4   medium tomatoes, quartered
     2   zucchini, cored and julienned
     6   new red potatoes, cooked and sliced
    ½   pound Gruyère, Cheddar, or mozzarella, grated
     1   head broccoli, cut into florets
     1   head cauliflower, cut into florets
     1   bunch parsley, chopped
         vinaigrette for dressing

Have all salad ingredients ready for assembly, except for the cauliflower and broccoli. Fill a large saucepan with water and bring to a boil. Then blanch the cauliflower for 3 to 4 minutes and the broccoli for 1½ minutes. Remove and run under cold water. Fill a large salad bowl half full of a mixture of the three lettuces. Arrange all the vegetables, except the potatoes, in colorful groupings on the lettuce and fan the potatoes over top. Sprinkle with cheese and parsley, and serve. Pass the vinaigrette on the side in a separate bowl.

Blanching is a "fast-cook" method used to soften and tenderize vegetables, and to get rid of the raw taste. In some cases, blanching will precede further cooking by another method. Blanching requires quickly immersing vegetables in just-boiling water, then dropping them into a colander, and running them under cold water to stop further cooking and to retain full color. Use a pot large enough so the vegetables won't be crowded, fill it with water and add a pinch of salt and ½ teaspoon lemon juice. Bring this to a slow boil. Add the vegetables, return to a simmer, then lower the temperature so that the water is motionless, as with poaching. Cook them briefly (see following time guidelines), put them in a colander, and shock them with cold water. Make sure all steam escapes by moving the vegetables around with your hands. They are then ready to use. We suggest the following blanching times for the vegetables used in our recipes: string beans, 2 to 2½ minutes (in winter, tougher beans may take up to 3 minutes); broccoli florets, 1½ minutes; carrots: julienned, immediately after the water comes back to a simmer; chunked, 3 to 4 minutes; circles, 1 minute; asparagus, average-sized stalks, 5 to 8 minutes; cauliflower, 3 to 4 minutes; corn on the cob, 5 to 8 minutes (with corn on the cob, add 1 cup of milk to the water before cooking).

Every part of the delicious vegetable broccoli is usable, including the tough stalk, but you must cut it up into bite-size pieces first. Start by paring the florets off the head. To do this, cut off each floret, leaving just a small stalk at the base. This will look like a miniature bouquet of green flowers. Then, trim off the bottom of each "bouquet" into a pointed arrow shape, because the small stems would otherwise take longer to cook than the florets. This way they cook uniformly. Trim off any leaves. If the floret "bouquet" is overly large, slice it in half lengthwise.

To trim the stalk, cut off both the flowering and the stem end. Stand this trimmed stalk on end, and slice the skin off all four sides. The inner portion is tender, tasting like water chestnuts, and can be readily sliced into coin shapes for cooking with the florets.

〰〰〰〰〰〰〰〰〰〰〰〰〰〰〰〰〰〰〰〰〰〰〰〰〰〰〰〰〰〰

Salads can be delicious, especially here in the United States where there are so many different kinds of lettuces. We feel very strongly about having the proper balance of textures and tastes, so for our salads, we combine Boston, Romaine, red-leaf and curly (green-leaf) lettuces—and watercress. As you will find, different varieties of lettuces can be combined for interesting dishes.

All lettuce must be handled with care: it should be well cleaned, cut and well dried to fully appreciate the flavor. Preparing lettuce is fun and actually soothing, once you get into the proper rhythm. Tear all leaves into bite-sized pieces for easy eating, and to prevent dressing from dribbling. It's taboo to cut any lettuce except Romaine, since the soft leaves turn color quickly.

To ready all lettuces except Romaine, cut off the core end and tear the leaf off the spine by ripping it into pieces, starting at the top of the head. To ready Romaine, you should use a thin boning knife to cut off the core end. Then, in a motion rather like the wrist motion used when swinging a squash racquet, cut the leaf into equal pieces. Discard the tough central spine, which is also very sandy.

Once the leaves are torn into pieces, put them into a colander or a clean sink, and rinse well in cold water. Dry leaves thoroughly in a salad spinner or in a colander lined with paper towels. (Wet leaves keep dressings from clinging.) Wrap the leaves in dry towels and refrigerate *until half an hour before serving time. Too-chilled lettuce is unpleasant and tasteless.*

VEAL AND TOMATO SALAD

SERVES 6 TO 8

One evening we prepared a delicious veal Provençal and decided at lunch next day to try out a veal salad with the leftovers. What we came up with is this Provençal-like salad, with freshly chopped vegetables and a dressing, served on a bed of spinach.

3½ pound boneless veal roast, cooked, trimmed and cubed
¼ cup basil leaves, julienned
1½ pounds Gruyère cheese, julienned
1½ cups cherry tomatoes, halved or quartered, depending on size
2 cups pitted black olives
1 cup walnut pieces
2 bunches fresh spinach, trimmed, cleaned and dried

DRESSING

1 tablespoon Dijon mustard
½ cup sweet white wine
1 teaspoon lemon juice
1 teaspoon wine vinegar
2 teaspoons kosher salt
2 teaspoons white pepper
1 cup olive oil, or to taste

Combine veal with basil, Gruyère, tomatoes, olives, and walnut pieces, and place on a bed of spinach. To make dressing, whisk together mustard, wine, lemon juice, vinegar, salt and pepper. Whisk in oil to taste. Pour dressing on salad, and toss to combine.

CHICKEN SALAD PROVENÇAL

O ur customers adore our chicken salads—each one we make calls for moist, meaty chunks of poached chicken breast. We often dress the meat while it is still warm so it absorbs the flavors and moisture of the dressing. Versatile white meat can adapt to so many different flavors, and we have served every kind of chicken salad imaginable. But our Chicken Salad Provençal is probably in the most demand.

4 whole chicken breasts, skinned, cleaned, fillets removed and reserved
3 cups halved cherry tomatoes
2 cups halved canned artichoke hearts
1½ cups halved pitted black olives
3 small zucchini, striped, halved lengthwise, thinly sliced on the diagonal
2 pounds cooked new potatoes, quartered

DRESSING

2 cups mayonnaise
1 cup sour cream
1 tablespoon Dijon mustard
1 tablespoon kosher salt
2 teaspoons ground white pepper

2 teaspoons paprika
¼ cup lemon juice (juice of 1 lemon)
¼ cup white wine
½ cup olive oil

Poach chicken breasts following directions highlighted on page 69. Poach for 11 minutes.

While chicken is poaching, make dressing: First whisk mayonnaise and sour cream in a bowl, then mustard, salt, pepper, and paprika, then lemon juice and wine. Drizzle in olive oil, whisking constantly.

Three minutes before chicken is done, add reserved fillets. Drain chicken and cut into strips.

Combine chicken, tomatoes, artichoke hearts, olives, zucchini and potatoes. Stir in dressing, mixing well. Refrigerate salad 1 hour to allow flavors to blend, but serve at room temperature.

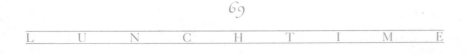

Poaching is a delicate way to cook food, because once the food is in the warm poaching water, the water never moves. This prevents overcooking and demolishing the outside shape, and undercooking the inside. Always remember to keep the heat low. Poaching liquid should contain all the necessary ingredients to flavor vegetables, seafood, chicken or meat. For fruits, the poaching liquid should be sweet and syrupy. Cooking time depends on what you want to poach. See individual recipes for timing.

STUFFED AVOCADOS

SERVES
6

½ cup white wine
1 tablespoon chopped fresh sage or 1½ teaspoons dried
1 tablespoon chopped fresh parsley
6 black peppercorns
1 bay leaf
1 teaspoon kosher salt
½ lemon
¼ cup sweet butter, melted
1 pound medium sea scallops, cleaned
1 pound large shrimp, cleaned, shelled and halved
1 bunch broccoli, cut in florets
1 yellow squash, peeled lightly so it will still be yellow, cored and julienned
¾ cup Mustard Vinaigrette (recipe on page 62)
¼ pound cherry tomatoes, halved
3 avocados, halved lengthwise, pits removed
red-leaf lettuce for decoration, washed, dried and torn in half

Combine wine, sage, parsley, peppercorns, bay leaf and salt in a saucepan over medium heat. Add a squeeze of lemon juice and then the lemon. Bring to a boil, then lower to a simmer and continue until liquid has been reduced by half. Add scallops and shrimp and cook 2 minutes. Remove from heat. Keep seafood in hot liquid 2 minutes, turning occasionally. Place the seafood in bowl, reserving liquid.

Heat enough water in a saucepan to cook broccoli and squash. Add a pinch of salt and a few drops of lemon juice. Bring to a boil. Add broccoli and cook 20 seconds; add squash and simmer 10 seconds longer. Drain in colander and shock under cold water. While still tepid, place vegetables in bowl with the scallops and shrimp. Add the vinaigrette; strain the broth from the seafood and add to the bowl. Add tomatoes and mix with hands.

Place an avocado half on a bed of red-leaf lettuce on each plate. Fill avocado halves evenly with the prepared mixture.

Sandwiches

A classic, immortal lunch food, the sandwich can take as many forms—layered or flat, grilled or chilled—and contain as many ingredients, as imagination, space and pocketbook allow. It's hard to say which should hold the limelight—a textured bread or roll, the fillings, or a zesty sandwich spread.

The sandwich menu at Good Enough to Eat is limited, but, we feel, unusual. Each bite, each mouthful, of any of our sandwiches turns up different consistencies and tastes. In addition, there's always a crunchiness from watercress or a leafy green. By and large, our customers are delighted by our creative combinations, and that's what a sandwich should be all about.

Because of their texture and character, we've included 2 breads we often slice up for our sandwiches.

FRENCH BREAD OR ROLLS

M A K E S
1 LOAF
OR 2
4 OZ. ROLLS

½ cup plus 2 tablespoons warm water
½ ounce compressed yeast or ¾ package dry yeast
    pinch of sugar
2 cups all-purpose flour plus additional flour for
    kneading
1½ teaspoons salt
2 tablespoons olive oil
¼ cup white cornmeal
1 egg yolk mixed with 1 tablespoon water

Place warm water in measuring cup; add yeast and sugar. Let sit 10 minutes, covered, until foamy.

Place 2 cups flour and the salt into a large bowl. Pour proofed yeast mixture into flour; add salt and oil. When combined, turn dough out onto floured kneading surface and knead about 15 minutes, adding flour if necessary, until dough is firm and elastic and springs back when dough is flattened with fist. Bring edges into center, making a knob when you press it with your finger.

Wipe out bowl and oil it. Place dough in the bowl, turn to coat with oil, cover with plastic or clean towel, and let rise in warm place until double in bulk, about 40 minutes to 1 hour. Punch down dough.

Sprinkle cornmeal on cookie sheet.

Form dough into a rectangle 7 to 8 inches long by 2 to 3 inches wide. Roll up as for jelly roll, making sure edges are tucked in. Pinch the seams and place on cornmeal-sprinkled cookie sheet.

To make French rolls instead of bread, divide dough in two. Flatten dough with palms of hand into 3-inch circle. Gather up all edges of circle and bring toward center. Holding on to gathered dough, make circular motions in order to smooth dough into small round roll. Be sure after gathering you have pinched edges together tightly.

Preheat oven to 375 degrees.

Brush egg wash on bread; with a sharp knife, make 2 to 3 slits in the loaf, or 1 slit on each roll. Let bread rise for about 45 minutes, until doubled in bulk.

Just before putting bread in oven, spray it with water from a plant mister for an especially crunchy crust. Bake bread 20 to 25 minutes, until golden, spraying bread every 10 mintues.

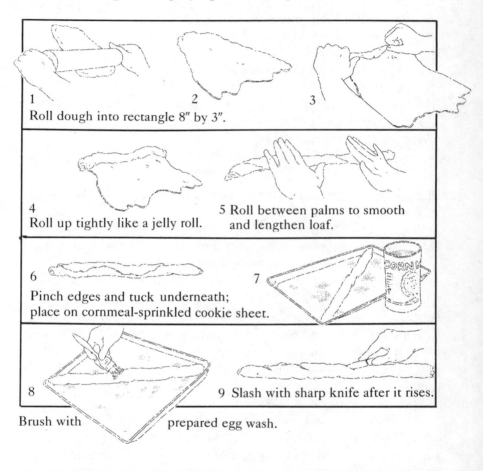

1
Roll dough into rectangle 8″ by 3″.

2

3

4
Roll up tightly like a jelly roll.

5 Roll between palms to smooth and lengthen loaf.

6
Pinch edges and tuck underneath; place on cornmeal-sprinkled cookie sheet.

7

8
Brush with   prepared egg wash.

9 Slash with sharp knife after it rises.

Most likely, you'll get much joy out of mixing and kneading bread dough. You may make several mistakes before you become good at it, but don't get discouraged. Baking is very personal, and when you love it and feel confident, you can make many wonderful things. Have patience, and later you can be experimental. In the meantime you will have more success with our simple recipes. A general tip for baking bread is to be sure to use tin bread pans and to grease them well before putting in the dough. Also, wash them after each use, and be sure to dry them well or they will rust or discolor.

A word about baking yeast breads: most novice cooks are afraid of making these breads, but they shouldn't be. Cooking with dry yeast is really a no-fail method. You'll know that the kneaded dough is ready for a second rising, or to form into loaves, when you can stick your finger in it and your finger springs right back. Also, the dough surface will feel silky and smooth.

WHOLE WHEAT BREAD 1 LOAF

- 2 tablespoons milk
- 1 cup water
- ¾ package dry yeast
- 2 teaspoons molasses
- 1½ cups all-purpose flour, plus additional flour for kneading
- 1 cup whole wheat flour
- ¾ cup old-fashioned rolled oats
- 2 teaspoons salt
- 2 tablespoons bran (optional)
- 2 tablespoons sweet butter, melted
- 1 egg yolk beaten with 2 tablespoons milk

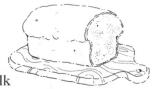

Lightly grease large bowl and 5-by-8-inch bread pan. Warm milk and 1 cup water in small saucepan over low heat until small bubbles appear around the edges. Pour into small bowl. Test with your finger to make sure it is not too hot (it should feel comfortably warm to the touch), then add the yeast and the molasses. Let it sit 10 minutes until foamy.

In a large bowl, combine flours, oats, salt and bran (if using). Add the butter and work lightly into dry ingredients. After yeast has proofed, add it to the flour-butter mixture until well incorporated.

Spread some additional all-purpose flour on kneading surface. Knead dough, incorporating up to 1 cup additional all-purpose flour. The dough should be soft but firm and elastic. Place dough in greased bowl, turning to coat all sides, then cover and let rise in a warm place about 1 hour, or until doubled in bulk. Punch down bread and place it in the prepared baking pan. Cover and let rise again for 45 minutes to 1 hour, until again doubled in bulk.

Preheat oven to 350 degrees.

Bake bread until browned on top and the bottom sounds hollow.

SLOPPY JOES AND SPINACH SALAD

SERVES

6

A family favorite, this sandwich lives up to its name. With the accompanying spinach salad, this becomes a filling lunch, satisfying enough for dinner, too.

  1 large onion, chopped
  1 green bell pepper, chopped
  3 tablespoons vegetable oil
  ¼ teaspoon chili powder
  ¼ teaspoon cayenne
  ½ teaspoon kosher salt
  1 teaspoon ground white pepper
  ½ teaspoon paprika
  3 pounds ground beef
  2 teaspoons Worcestershire sauce
1¼ cups ketchup
  1 teaspoon hot sauce
  ½ teaspoon dried basil
  1 cup corn kernels
  1 tablespoon Dijon mustard
  6 soft sandwich rolls or 12 slices of white bread

Sweat the onion and bell pepper in oil in a 10-inch skillet over very low heat, with chili powder, cayenne, salt, ground pepper and paprika, and simmer 15 minutes, until onions and bell peppers are soft. Transfer vegetables to a small bowl. Add beef to the same pan and brown it completely over medium heat, breaking up lumps with spoon. Stir in remaining ingredients, return reserved vegetables to the pan and simmer 30 minutes, stirring regularly so the meat does not burn.

Halve rolls and place them on dinner plates (or place 2 slices of bread on each plate). Spoon equal portions of meat mixture over each roll or bread slice. Serve Spinach Salad (recipe below) at side of plate. Supply lots of napkins.

Mushrooms deserve particular attention, so we've supplied some helpful hints about their preparation. Never, ever wash mushrooms. To clean them, just use a damp cloth moistened with cold water and a squeeze of lemon juice. The acid in the juice keeps them from discoloring. Cut off the very end of the stem, just at the bottom where it widens and is brown. To tournée mushrooms, which makes their caps look like chrysanthemums—lovely for garnish—hold the cap tightly in one hand and, with a sharp paring knife, make even grooves with a fast whittling motion all around the cap.

SPINACH SALAD

  1 small red onion, halved and thinly sliced
 ½ pound mushrooms, cleaned and either thinly sliced or tournéed
  1 cup drained black beans
 ¼ cup sharp Vermont Cheddar cheese, julienned or cubed
  1 pound fresh spinach, washed, dried, leaves cut in half

DRESSING

YIELDS
1¼ CUP

  1 cup vegetable oil
  2 tablespoons soy sauce
     juice of 1 lemon
 ½ to 1 teaspoon white pepper

(continued on next page)

Mix all salad ingredients, except the spinach, in a mixing bowl. Combine all dressing ingredients in a large measuring cup, stirring well. If they separate, don't worry. Stir to recombine. Place spinach on one side of the luncheon plate, using it as a bed for the rest of the salad ingredients. Drizzle the dressing over top.

ROAST BEEF, BRIE AND BACON SANDWICH WITH POTATO SALAD

SERVES
4

    8 slices whole wheat bread, sliced
    2 tablespoons Dijon or coarse-grain mustard
    1 bunch watercress, washed and dried
   12 slices cooked sugar-cured bacon, halved
    8 ounces Brie with rind, sliced
   ¾ pound thinly sliced Roast Beef (recipe follows)

Place 8 slices bread on board. Spread evenly with mustard. Divide watercress among 4 slices of bread; top with bacon, Brie and roast beef. Cover with remaining slices of bread and put on plate with the Potato Salad (recipe on page 77).

Roasting is a dry-heat cooking method suited to meats, poultry, vegetables and nuts. As in childhood, we still like our meats with a dark, crunchy exterior crust and rare inside. Often, we sear the outside to get that crust. The technique of searing is discussed on page 219. Or, we make a paste of mustard, cheeses, butter, spices and herbs to coat our meats to get the crust. Butter drizzled on the surface will also produce a crust.

ROAST BEEF

6-pound beef roast
2 to 4 tablespoons olive oil
1 tablespoon kosher salt
2 cloves garlic, minced

Preheat oven to 350 degrees.

Place beef in roaster. Rub on oil, salt and garlic. Roast 1 to 1¼ hours for medium-rare. Let roast sit 15 minutes before carving— or until cool for Roast Beef, Brie and Bacon Sandwich, above.

In our potato recipes—except for baking and mashing —we prefer using new red potatoes. They are sweet and have the perfect texture when cooked so many different ways. To prepare them, leave the skins on, making sure to cut all the black knots out. Put them into a large pot of cold water with a pinch of salt. Bring water to a boil. Then lower heat to a simmer (you will see only little bubbles in the water now) and never let the water boil again. Simmering is a gentle cooking method we find ideal for cooking potatoes through evenly. When tender, drain the potatoes in a colander and shock them with cold water. Use them as the recipe indicates.

POTATO SALAD

3 pounds new potatoes, unpeeled, scrubbed, cooked, and quartered
6 hard-cooked eggs, cut in wedges (page 83 for cooking eggs)
1 large red onion, chopped
2 green bell peppers, chopped
1 bunch scallions, sliced thinly

(continued on next page)

¾ cup Mayonnaise (see recipe page 63)
¾ cup sour cream
1 tablespoon coarse-grain mustard
¼ cup olive oil
2 tablespoons lemon juice
2 teaspoons kosher salt
2 teaspoons ground black pepper
1 teaspoon paprika
¼ cup chopped fresh parsley

Combine potatoes with the eggs. Add onion, bell peppers, and scallions. To make dressing, whisk mayonnaise, sour cream, mustard, oil, lemon juice, salt, pepper and paprika until well blended. Stir in parsley. Pour dressing over vegetables; mix gently until vegetables are well coated.

LE PAIN BAGNA

SERVES
4

This wonderful Provençal lunch sandwich, as popular in the south of France as pizza is in New York, is really a Niçoise salad heaped into a sandwich. In Provence, the hungry customer goes to a van, and asks a vendor to assemble the sandwich, stack the filling into an enormous hollowed-out roll. The filling is then covered with a rich "Almost Pesto" sauce, much like the one we describe here, and the entire sandwich is carefully wrapped up so the customer can walk to the nearest café, order a glass of red wine, and sit back to enjoy the wonderfully messy, delicious sandwich while people-watching.

6½-ounce can oil-packed tuna, or leftover fresh tuna
¼ cup olive oil
¼ cup mayonnaise
½ teaspoon lemon juice
2 large eggs, hard-cooked (see page 83)
4 large rolls (see page 71)
½ recipe Almost Pesto (page 182)
1 pound fresh spinach, washed and drained

2 medium beefsteak tomatoes, cored and thinly sliced
1 red onion, halved, and sliced as thin as possible
¼ pound Niçoise olives, pitted and halved
14-ounce can chickpeas, drained, marinated in 1 tablespoon lemon juice
4½-ounce jar marinated artichoke hearts, quartered
1 roasted red bell pepper (page 108), julienned
4 tablespoons freshly grated Parmesan cheese

Open the can of tuna; press out the oil. Place tuna in a bowl and flake. Mix in olive oil, mayonnaise and lemon juice.

Slice eggs in thin circles. Cut open the bread and remove a bit of the soft center. Spoon a little Almost Pesto on both halves of the bread. Then add spinach to both halves. Place remaining ingredients in even amounts on each roll, ending with the tuna mixture. Drizzle the sandwiches with the Almost Pesto sauce, close, and push down. Cut in half and serve on a plate with lots of paper napkins.

GRILLED HAM AND CHEESE SANDWICH, MACARONI SALAD

SERVES
4

*F*ew sandwiches are as satisfying as a grilled ham and cheese, here enlivened with a spread of tangy mustard and chewy dark bread. Its natural partner is a macaroni salad, a durable dish that is as at home on the dining-room table as on a picnic blanket.

½ pound mozzarella, cut into 8 thin slices
¼ cup plus 2 tablespoons olive oil
½ teaspoon kosher salt
pinch of ground pepper
4 fresh basil leaves, julienned, or 2 teaspoons dried
1 clove garlic, minced

8 slices whole wheat or other dark bread
4 tablespoons Dijon mustard
1 pound sliced smoked ham
2 plum tomatoes, thinly sliced
8 sprigs watercress

(continued on next page)

To the mozzarella slices add ¼ cup olive oil, the salt, pepper and basil. Allow to marinate 20 to 30 minutes. Preheat griddle.

Combine garlic with remaining 2 tablespoons oil. Brush 1 side of each slice of bread with oil, then lightly grill on each side. Spread bread with mustard on oiled side. Place ham and 2 slices of cheese on each of 4 slices of bread. Add 3 slices of tomato and a sprig of watercress to each slice. Cover with remaining bread and cut sandwich in two. Serve with Macaroni Salad (page 81) on the side.

Cooking pasta is an easy task, producing some of the most delightful meals. Fill a large stockpot with water, ½ cup vegetable oil and a pinch of salt, and bring to a boil. Then add the pasta, stirring to keep the pieces separate. Boil for 4 to 12 minutes, or until the pasta is cooked all the way through, but not mushy and sticky. We prefer our pasta cooked al dente, which requires less cooking time. Then pour pasta into a colander to drain, running it under hot water to remove the starch. Combine it with the appropriate sauce, according to the recipe, and serve right away. If you are not using the pasta immediately, run under cold water to stop the cooking, put it into a bowl and drizzle with olive oil.

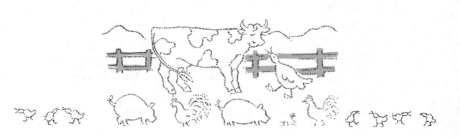

MACARONI SALAD

dill

- ½ pound ziti or rotelle
- 1 red onion, chopped
- 1 green pepper, chopped
- 1 red pepper, chopped
- 10 cherry tomatoes, sliced in half
- 2 tablespoons fresh dill, minced
- 2 tablespoons parsley, chopped
- ½ cup drained canned corn kernels
- ¼ cup Mayonnaise (recipe page 63)
- ¼ cup sour cream
- 1 teaspoon salt
- ½ teaspoon black pepper
- ½ teaspoon mustard
  dash of paprika

Cook pasta, combine remaining ingredients and toss well with pasta. Chill for at least 30 minutes.

CURRIED EGG SALAD SANDWICH WITH HERBED CHERRY TOMATO AND AVOCADO SALAD

*H*ardly any delicatessen or gourmet take-out would fail to offer their version of this classic, the egg salad sandwich. We love it too, and accent the egg mixture with a dash of curry powder. An Indian egg salad sandwich? We serve ours with a light salad featuring cherry tomatoes and avocado on the side.

6 large eggs, hard-cooked (see box)
2 tablespoons melted clarified butter
1 teaspoon salt
1 tablespoon curry powder
1 teaspoon white pepper
½ teaspoon cumin
½ teaspoon paprika
¼ teaspoon dry mustard
½ teaspoon minced garlic
½ cup Mayonnaise (see recipe page 63)
½ cup sour cream
3 scallions, thinly sliced
3 slices bacon, cooked and crumbled
1 head red-leaf lettuce, washed and dried
1 loaf Dill Bread (recipe page 18) or 12 slices dark bread

Place butter in skillet over medium heat. Add curry powder, white pepper, cumin, paprika, dry mustard and the garlic; sauté 5 to 6 minutes, then remove from heat.

Whisk mayonnaise and sour cream together in a small bowl. Stir in scallions and bacon and, with a rubber spatula, scrape the spices into the dressing and mix well. Mash eggs with a fork and combine with this mixture. To assemble the sandwich, layer lettuce leaves on a bottom slice of bread, spread on the egg mixture, then put on the top slice. Serve with Herbed Cherry Tomato and Avocado Salad (below) on the side.

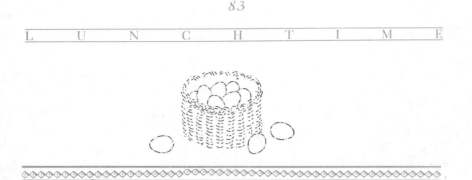

For hard-cooking eggs, fill a saucepan with water. Bring the water to a boil, then gently place eggs in the water and bring the water back to a boil. Reduce heat to a simmer for exactly 11 minutes. Do not let the water boil again. Immediately drain off the hot water and run the eggs under very cold water. When they are cool enough to handle, they may be peeled. This procedure prevents the yolk from changing color at the rim.

HERBED CHERRY TOMATO AND AVOCADO SALAD

SERVES
6

- 1 pound cherry tomatoes, halved, if large
- 1 ripe avocado, peeled, pit removed, cut in ½-inch cubes
  juice of 1 lemon
- 2 teaspoons kosher salt
- ½ cup olive oil
- 1 to 2 teaspoons julienned fresh basil leaves

Place tomatoes and avocado in bowl. Squeeze on the lemon juice, sprinkle with salt, gently mix in olive oil, being careful not to crush avocado cubes. Add basil to taste.

CRAB CAKES WITH TARTAR SAUCE, HOPPING JOHN, CELERY ROOT AND RED CABBAGE RAVE

SERVES
8

These yummy crab cakes can be enjoyed either as a sandwich filling or solo. Either way, spread with our Tartar Sauce. For an extra-Southern taste, we serve these with Hopping John, a dish consisting of rice, ham and black-eyed peas (see page 85). But, back to New England again, we also accompany them with a coleslaw-like dish calling for that gnarly but delicious vegetable, celery root.

 4   stalks celery
 1   red onion, chopped
 4   tablespoons sweet butter, melted
 1   pound potatoes, peeled, cooked and mashed
 2   pounds lump crabmeat, picked over
 ½   cup unflavored bread crumbs
 1   tablespoon lemon juice
 2   tablespoons Mayonnaise (see recipe page 63)
 ¼   cup chopped fresh parsley
 1   teaspoon kosher salt
 ½   teaspoon white pepper
 1   teaspoon paprika
 2   teaspoons hot pepper sauce
 2   eggs, lightly beaten
     vegetable oil for frying

Sauté celery and onion in butter until soft. Set aside to cool.

Combine remaining ingredients except for eggs and oil. Add sautéed celery and onion to mixture. Mix in eggs until well combined. Form into 16 round cakes; place on cookie sheet and refrigerate for 30 to 45 minutes, until firm.

Meanwhile, preheat oil to 300 degrees. Place 4 cakes at a time into oil. Fry 7 to 8 minutes, turning once, until golden. Place on paper towels to drain; keep warm in oven set at 200 degrees while frying remaining cakes.

TARTAR SAUCE

- 1 cup Mayonnaise (recipe page 63)
- 1 teaspoon fresh lemon juice
- 1 tablespoon Dijon mustard
- 1 teaspoon kosher salt
- ½ teaspoon white pepper
- ¼ cup fresh parsley, chopped
- 2 small scallions, thinly sliced
- 2 tablespoons drained capers (optional)
- 6 chopped pickles (gherkins)
- 2 tablespoons juice from pickles

Place mayonnaise in bowl with lemon juice (if you are using store-bought mayonnaise, add 2 teaspoons fresh lemon juice rather than 1, and 2 tablespoons olive oil). Add mustard, salt, pepper, parsley, scallions and capers, if using. Whisk well, then add chopped pickles and the pickle juice. Serve in individual ramekins.

HOPPING JOHN

- 1 medium onion, chopped
- 4 tablespoons sweet butter
- 1½ teaspoons kosher salt
- 1 teaspoon white pepper
- 1 tablespoon hot pepper sauce
- ¾ pound smoked ham, cubed, or 1 ham hock
- 2 cups long-grain rice
- 1½ cups dried black-eyed peas, cooked according to package instructions

If you are using a ham hock, it should be put in a small pot and covered with water and cooked for 30 minutes. Sauté onion in butter with salt, pepper, hot pepper sauce, and cubed ham or hock over medium heat 10 to 15 minutes, until onion is soft and ham is hot. Add rice and sauté 5 minutes. Add amount of water as directed on rice box. Bring to a boil, reduce heat, cover and cook till water is absorbed. Add peabeans and cook 5 minutes longer. If using ham hock, remove bone and shred any meat into the rice, stirring to combine.

CELERY ROOT AND RED CABBAGE RAVE

SERVES
8

1½ pounds celery root, peeled
1¼ medium heads red cabbage, shredded
  1 egg yolk
¼ cup Dijon mustard
1½ teaspoons kosher salt
  1 teaspoon white pepper
  2 tablespoons fresh lemon juice
  1 tablespoon white wine
  2 cups olive oil
  1 tablespoon caraway seeds

Place the celery root and cabbage
in a mixing bowl. Then mix in
the remaining ingredients. Prepare the dressing, following
procedure for making Mayonnaise on page 63. Pour the dressing
over the vegetables and let them macerate for at least 2 hours.

Afternoon Tea

This tradition is taken very seriously in Europe, especially in Britain: The milk must be heated to just the right temperature and the water boiled, but not overboiled. The tea must steep for just the correct time. Jams must be chunky, and the clotted cream very fresh. The afternoon tea is so important that everyone, busy executives included, can find time to stop and enjoy it.

But, alas, afternoon tea is rarely observed here. Too bad, because it provides a mid-afternoon chance to socialize, eat well, and break the tedium of the workaday world. Unlike cocktails, which can numb the senses, afternoon teas relax people without making them sleepy and provide a pickup that truly refreshes.

Perhaps the correct way to approach this civilized time out is to think of it as similar to the morning coffee break, when a freshly brewed beverage is served, sometimes with a plate or tray of baked goods or finger sandwiches. Although the afternoon tea can become a daily habit, it also provides the format for very special intimate parties.

SCONES

**YIELDS
12 SCONES**

Scones, the traditional tea bread, must be moist and sturdy so they will not crumble when smothered with clotted cream and strawberry jam.

4 cups all-purpose flour	2 large eggs, lightly beaten
1/4 cup sugar	1 cup buttermilk, chilled
2 tablespoons baking powder	1/2 cup raisins
3/4 cup sweet butter, chilled	1 large egg beaten with 1 tablespoon
1/4 teaspoon baking soda	water for wash

(continued on next page)

Preheat oven to 350 degrees.

Combine flour, sugar and baking powder and soda in a large bowl. Cut in the butter, working the flour through fingers until it resembles large peas. Make a well in the center of the flour mixture and pour the eggs and buttermilk into it. Stir well to combine, then gradually add the raisins. Mix the dough with the hands and bring it together to form a ball.

Turn the dough out onto a lightly floured board and gently bring it together for a few minutes. Flatten the dough with the palms of your hands until it is uniformly 1 inch thick. Dip a 2½-inch scalloped-edge biscuit cutter into the flour, then cut scones out and place them on the baking sheet, about 2 inches apart. Brush with egg wash. Bake for about 30 to 35 minutes, or until scones are golden.

CLOTTED CREAM

SERVES
4

T *his closely resembles the British product, but we can't make an exact replica because the proper cream is unavailable in this country. Sweet and creamy, with a subtle tang, this clotted cream is like whipped buttermilk. Beware —it's very fattening.*

  1 *cup heavy sweet cream*
 ¼ *cup sour cream*
    pinch of confectioner's sugar

In mixing bowl, start whisking the sweet cream, and when it thickens and light peaks form, whisk in sour cream and sugar. Beat until thick but still spoonable and soft.

3

DINNERTIME

*I*f breakfasts sharpen the senses, dinners should comfort and lull them. But the homey foods people seek at day's end should never be so gentle or so predictable that they bore. Yes, the day should end on a softer note than it began, but the sensuous tastes of the evening meal should linger in the memory long after lights out.

Dinners at Good Enough to Eat follow that formula. We start with basic family foods familiar to most of us, then spin our menus off from there. Many factors influence the final shape of each meal—other recipes and other cuisines, other restaurants and other cooks, a tour of the markets and a tour of our collective food memories. The results of our culinary meanderings? What starts as a commonplace entree of southern fried chicken may end up wearing a cloak of Mexican chili and be complemented by an amalgam of ethnic side dishes, all colorful and festive, and all working together. We've learned to trust our  sense of adventure—following our crusty outside-mushy inside theory—so that our home-style meals, while not *exactly* what Granny would have served, will always delight, and possibly shock, the taste buds. Many of our patrons enjoy this playfulness, and since we change our menu every night, they will phone us in the afternoon to see what unusual dinners we have planned.

Likewise, we urge home cooks to experiment with, and get excited about, planning dinners for their families and for themselves. More than for any other meal, you can bend cooking rules to borrow a taste from one cuisine, a technique from another, a special ingredient from a third. If you follow some common-sense rules, what you create will be tantalizing. First and foremost, no dinner (and no meal) should be so bizarre or trendy that its various components make no culinary sense. You must carefully avoid too many combinations, too many tastes. We recall a particularly fancy dinner party where the hosts served a delicate rack of lamb with heavy, sweet baked beans—terrible. Always remember, flavors and textures should mesh—never clash or overpower one another.

For best results, follow the seasons, buying and using the freshest ingredients available, and substituting if what you want is not available at top quality. Clearly you would not plan on pumpkin pie in June, or serve less-than-perfect strawberries. We rarely use costly, exotic or scarce ingredients, because they take away from the home-cooked feeling we strive for. We also keep complementary tastes in mind. For instance, fatty lamb needs something tart and fruity to cut any disagreeable residual fattiness, so we may serve a lamb roast with a plum-peach relish. Versatile pork and chicken, on the other hand, because they are so neutral, can stand up to tangy blandishments, and our toppings or extras can range from poached, spiced fruit to hot, sour mustard sauces.

As artisans, cooks need an eye for color and design, elements we always consider when planning a meal. We, too, work with an almost unlimited artist's palette: our foods; and a canvas of sorts: each dinner plate. We're careful that the dishes in our meals are 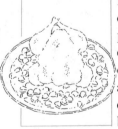 not all the same color—we would not serve a white cream sauce and scalloped potatoes on the same plate, for example. We plan that the natural shape of attractive ingredients somehow stands out—for example, we place clumps of broccoli florets against a contrasting background so that their tufted ends catch the eye. We carefully pare and slice vegetables and fruits to highlight their symmetry. Have you ever really studied a cross section of a cucumber or a carrot? Also, by staying within the inside rim of the dinner plate, we create a framed food painting. Within that constricted circular border, we arrange the food so its lines follow the curve of the plate—the

overall effect is often a fanciful pinwheel. But we never target the
center with such accents as a stemmed cherry or a black olive. As
a final garnish, we often brighten each plate with a bouquet of
trimmed watercress and a lemon wedge, one side dipped in
chopped parsley, the other in paprika.

Since we see our patrons as part of our extended family, we
always serve substantial portions—our mound theory, once again.
We do want them to have room for our family desserts, which is
why we never serve an appetizer course, but they may have to
readjust their belts, or linger over coffee, before ordering chocolate
cake.

We have organized this chapter into
three main categories—meat, poultry,
and seafood—to offer a variety of dinner
meals.

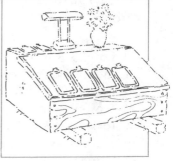

In general, side
dishes can readily be
interchanged from one
meal to another.

*We accompany many of our main courses at lunch and
dinner with mayonnaise-based vegetable dishes, or rel-
ishes. For convenience and the best flavor, prepare, dress
and chill these dishes for several hours before serving.
This allows time for the flavors to mingle and develop.
But do not serve the dish straight from the refrigerator
or its full flavor will be muted: at least one hour before
serving, remove from refrigerator to bring the dish to
room temperature.*

CORN RELISH

A t Good Enough to Eat, each dinner begins with a relish platter, a New England tradition which Ann loves. We use this in place of an appetizer or soup, and this relish plate occupies patrons until dinner is served. Its ingredients change, depending on the season, but each mixture is rich in color and texture. After the relish we serve a green salad with seasonal toppings and a basket of freshly sliced homemade French Bread (see page 71) served with a ramekin of sweet butter.

1¼ pounds firm zucchini, cleaned and diced
   1 medium-sized red onion, chopped
1½ cups canned corn kernels, drained
   1 teaspoon black pepper
1½ teaspoons kosher salt
   ¼ teaspoon sugar, optional
   ½ cup vegetable oil

Combine all ingredients in a large mixing bowl, stirring to mix well, then refrigerate for at least 4 hours before serving. At dinner-time, place a mounded spoonful of relish on a salad plate and serve it with a handful of crisp croutons and a ramekin of cottage cheese. To make the croutons, which you can prepare a day ahead and keep fresh wrapped in plastic, slice a loaf of French bread as thinly as possible, preferably ours. Brush each slice with melted butter that has been salted and seasoned with minced garlic if desired. Place each slice on a cookie sheet, and brown in a 350-degree oven for 15 to 20 minutes.

Meat Meals

PORK LOIN

in

PAPRIKA SAUCE

SOUR CREAM PARMESAN POTATOES

PEAR SUCCOTASH

SERVES

8 TO 10

When Carrie and her husband were honeymooning, they craved pork in any form—chops, roast, ribs, tenderloins. Because they both love to dream up new recipes, they started out with a pork loin, then thought of all the ingredients that combine well with pork: fruit, paprika, lima beans, sour cream, potatoes and cheese. Each of these suggested some element of this meal, their final creation. Of course, they carried out our crunchy-mushy theme. The paprika sauce crusts the pork, and the baked cheese crusts the potatoes. What's mushy. The pear succotash.

PORK LOIN IN
PAPRIKA SAUCE

SERVES
8 TO 10

    5-pound loin of pork, boned and tied, about ½ loin
    Paprika Sauce (recipe follows)

Preheat oven to 350 degrees.
   Place pork in roaster. Prick about 12 ½-inch-deep holes around the flesh with paring knife. When sauce is ready, spread it over the loin, making sure the entire loin is covered.

For cooking, you absolutely do not need a costly wine. We found out in cooking school, after making many taste tests, that any basic cheap wine will do fine, since most of the liquor evaporates.

PAPRIKA SAUCE

MAKES
6 CUPS

  2 tablespoons sweet butter
  2 tablespoons bacon fat or 2 tablespoons olive oil
  3 large onions, thinly sliced
  4 medium cloves garlic, minced
1½ teaspoons salt
1½ teaspoons ground black pepper
  3 tablespoons paprika
⅛ teaspoon cayenne
¾ cup red wine
½ cup beef stock
    13-ounce can crushed tomatoes
    13-ounce can plum tomatoes with liquid, crushed
  2 tablespoons tomato paste
½ tablespoon brown sugar
  1 tablespoon chopped fresh thyme, or 1½ teaspoons dried
  1 teaspoon dried basil

Heat butter and fat; sauté onion, garlic, salt, pepper, paprika and cayenne over medium heat until onions are light brown, about 5 minutes. Deglaze the pan with the wine, then reduce by half again, about 10 minutes. Stir in remaining ingredients. Simmer, stirring often, 15 to 20 minutes.

SOUR CREAM PARMESAN POTATOES

SERVES
8 TO 10

1½ cups sour cream
  1 tablespoon kosher salt
  2 teaspoons ground white pepper
  ¼ teaspoon hot pepper sauce
  1 teaspoon paprika
  ½ teaspoon dry mustard
  1 teaspoon powdered thyme
  ½ cup sweet butter, melted
  4 pounds new potatoes, scrubbed and quartered
  1 to 2 cups freshly grated Parmesan cheese

Preheat oven to 350 degrees.

Combine sour cream, salt, pepper, hot pepper sauce, paprika, mustard, thyme and butter in mixing bowl. Add potatoes and stir to coat well.

Spread mixture on baking sheet and sprinkle Parmesan cheese over top. Bake 30 to 40 minutes, until potatoes are brown.

PEAR SUCCOTASH

SERVES
8 TO 10

3 to 4 slices thick-cut bacon, cut again into ½-inch pieces
1 medium onion, chopped
2 cloves garlic, minced
½ teaspoon kosher salt
½ teaspoon coarsely ground black pepper
½ teaspoon cayenne
½ cup beef broth
½ cup heavy cream
   11-ounce can corn kernels, drained
   10-ounce package frozen lima beans, thawed
3 large pears, slightly underripe, peeled, cored and cut in
   1-inch cubes

Sauté bacon until crisp, about 7 minutes. Remove bacon, drain and place in bowl. Discard all but ¼ cup bacon fat.

Add onion, garlic, salt, pepper and cayenne to bacon fat in pan. Sauté until onions are soft and lightly golden; be careful not to burn the garlic.

Add broth and reduce the liquid by half, about 10 to 12 minutes.

Meanwhile, in a small saucepan, reduce the cream over medium heat by about half, swirling the saucepan regularly.

Combine the corn and lima beans with the onion mixture and add the cream. Stir in the bacon and add the pears, and simmer 5 to 10 minutes longer until the mixture thickens enough to coat the back of a spoon. (If the pears are very hard, add them a few minutes before adding the corn and lima beans.)

Taste the flavor of home-cooked food and feel the intimacy and warmth of mealtime in these colorful illustrations that evoke memories of the delights and securities of childhood, of traditions with friends and family, and of the celebration and joy of food that *Good Enough to Eat* recaptures with its recipes.

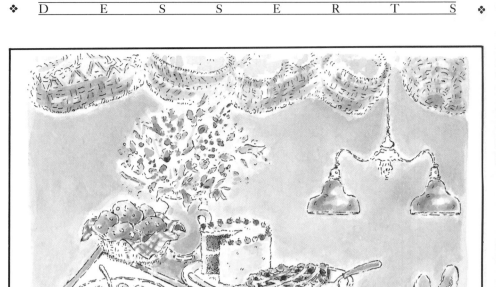

SAUTÉED CALF'S LIVER

with

GLAZED ONIONS
AND APPLE TOPPING

··

WHOLE BEETS
WITH LEAVES

··

BAKED POTATO
STUFFED

with

MASHED AVOCADO

SERVES Between the liver and beets with greens, this
healthful meal packs a mighty wallop. Splurge
___8___ on a good cut of calf's liver—its full, nutty taste
and buttery texture are worth the extra cost. Don't skimp
with less costly beef liver; the dish will not be the same. We
like our liver rare, so we cook it quickly. It is important to
serve this dish on warmed plates because liver gets cold fast.
Although we don't actually cook with it here (but we do use
it with the liver at the table), ketchup and its sweetness
inspired our onion dish. We cut the onions very thick, and
cook them slowly so they release all their natural sugars. To
achieve that same caramelized taste, some cooks sprinkle on
extra sugar. After cooking the onions, deglaze the pan, scraping up all the sugary pan juices, and pour these back on the
onions.

Beets are such a practical vegetable: you can use the leaves one night, the beets the next. Or, cook and serve them together, as with this recipe. This is probably Carrie's husband's favorite dish. The beautiful beet leaves are left intact, then sautéed and used as a bed for the cooked sliced beets. The overall taste is a little spicy, a little sugary.

The baked potato is delicious, and can be prepared ahead of time, to be warmed up while you prepare the rest of dinner. Avocado is delicious with liver and with potatoes, so mashing it for a potato stuffing seemed obvious.

SAUTÉED CALF'S LIVER WITH GLAZED ONIONS AND APPLE TOPPING

SERVES
8

TOPPING

- 4 tablespoons sweet butter
- 2 large Macintosh or Cortland apples, peeled, cored and sliced ⅛ inch thick
- 1 teaspoon kosher salt
- 1 teaspoon ground pepper
- ½ teaspoon paprika
- 2 large onions, halved and cut crosswise into ½-inch-thick slices
- ½ to 1 cup red wine
- 1 tablespoon brown sugar (optional)
- ¼ cup raisins soaked in ¼ cup warm red wine (optional)
- 8 strips crisp bacon, cut in ½-inch pieces (optional)

CALF'S LIVER

- 1 cup all-purpose flour
- ½ cup wheat germ
- 1 teaspoon kosher salt
- 1 teaspoon black pepper
- ½ teaspoon paprika
- 1 cup sweet butter
- 8 slices calf's liver, 8 to 9 ounces each

In French, sauter means "to jump," and that's what food cooked this way does: it jumps in a pan with clarified butter, or a combination of clarified butter and vegetable or olive oil, while you shake the pan on, or just over, high heat. Sautéing cooks meat and poultry quickly—overcooking causes membranes to break down and the food loses taste. We use a combination of oil and clarified butter for cooking meats and poultry because butter alone would burn too quickly and the meat would not cook through before the butter burned away. Figure on using 1 tablespoon of butter for 1 portion of food. Use a heavyish pan that conducts heat well, has slatted sides, and a sturdy handle. We don't recommend nonstick pans. They don't conduct heat well, and their finish always ends up peeling off. Make sure all vegetables are patted dry to avoid any splattering, and to remove any water from the vegetables, which also causes meat to burn. To turn meat or poultry, tilt the pan so the oil goes to the rear. Then, pick up the food with tongs, lifting it up toward you. Turn it over, replace in the pan, and continue cooking.

To make topping, melt 2 tablespoons butter in a large skillet and add apples. Sauté over medium heat 3 to 4 minutes, until apples are soft but still retain their shape. Remove apples to small bowl.

Add remaining 2 tablespoons butter to skillet and raise heat. Add salt, pepper and paprika. When butter is sizzling, add onions, separating into semicircles. Turn heat up high and shake pan 2 minutes, or until some onion sticks to bottom of the pan—then deglaze the pan with the wine. Continue shaking and deglazing pan 5 to 10 minutes, until onions are soft and golden brown. If onions have not browned, stir in the brown sugar to caramelize them. Add onions and any juices to the apples. Stir in raisins and bacon. Keep warm until ready to use.

In a large separate bowl, combine flour with wheat germ, salt, pepper and paprika.

Add 2 tablespoons butter for each slice of liver to the skillet over medium-high heat. Dredge liver in flour mixture and shake off excess. Add several slices of liver to the skillet without crowding. Shaking skillet constantly, cook liver 2 minutes each side for medium-rare, or longer according to taste. Repeat with remaining butter and liver. Put the liver on a plate and mound on the topping.

WHOLE BEETS WITH LEAVES

SERVES 8

3 bunches beets, leaves trimmed to within 1 inch of beets and reserved
½ cup firmly packed brown sugar
large onion, peeled, root left on
3 large cloves garlic, peeled
½ teaspoon ground cinnamon
2 tablespoons wine vinegar

Red wine vinegar is number 1 in our kitchen. We hardly ever use fruity or fancy imported vinegars.

---

1 tablespoon kosher salt
6 black peppercorns
⅓ cup hot pepper sauce
½ teaspoon red pepper flakes
2 bay leaves
½ teaspoon cayenne
½ teaspoon fresh, finely chopped ginger
1 tablespoon lemon juice
strip of lemon zest
3 tablespoons olive oil

Place beets in pot with water to see how much water is needed to cover them. Remove beets. You will have the right amount of water in the pot. Add remaining ingredients except oil to the water. Bring to a boil and simmer 20 to 30 minutes. Add beets and simmer until tender when pierced with a fork. Remove beets from pot, reserving 1 cup cooking liquid.

When beets are cool enough to handle, cut off stem base at tail and slip off skins. Slice beets in ½ inch rounds. Cover with reserved cooking liquid and 2 tablespoons olive oil and keep warm.

Wash the beet leaves thoroughly under running water. Heat remaining tablespoon oil in a skillet with a pinch of salt and a drop of wine vinegar. Add beet leaves and sauté, stirring 1 minute, until wilted. Drain the beets, reserving ¼ cup of liquid. Serve the beet leaves as a bed for the drained beets. Just before serving, deglaze the skillet with the reserved beet juice. Reduce to 1 tablespoon and pour over beets. Serve immediately.

The word deglaze comes from the French cooking term déglacer, to scrape up cooking juices, reduce them to a syrup and make them into a sauce. You should always use this sauce-enhancing method after sautéing, pan frying and searing. Food residue sticks in the pan, and these tasty little goodies—crunchy, brown, and loaded with flavor—should be scraped up before they burn and become bitter. To deglaze, pour liquid (wine, liquor, juice, cider, stock or water) right onto the sticking spots, and loosen them with a wooden spoon. Continue cooking and stirring over high heat and reduce the liquid to ¼ the original amount, or as recipe indicates. You can season these cooking juices however you wish, or make them into a cream sauce by adding heavy cream, lowering the heat, and stirring.

BAKED POTATO STUFFED WITH MASHED AVOCADO

4 large Idaho potatoes
1½ tablespoons olive oil
2 teaspoons kosher salt

STUFFING

small ripe avocado
1 cup sour cream
1 teaspoon kosher salt
1 teaspoon ground white pepper
pinch of cayenne
pinch of dry mustard
2 drops hot pepper sauce
juice of 1 large lemon
½ cup sweet butter, melted

TOPPING

¼ cup grated Cheddar
cheese
1 small red onion,
chopped
chopped fresh
coriander

Preheat oven to 350 degrees.

Rub potatoes with oil, sprinkle with salt, prick with a fork in several places, and bake 45 minutes to 1 hour, until done.

Slit the potatoes in half and scoop out the insides without tearing the skin. Mash potato, then add avocado and mash until blended. Beat in sour cream, spices, lemon juice and butter. Refill potato skins with mixture and sprinkle with cheese. Place in oven for 15 minutes before serving, then garnish with onion and coriander.

STUFFED CABBAGE WITH BUTTERED NOODLES

This classically sweet and savory dish comes from Ann's family. It really typifies Jewish cooking. "It tastes so traditional," said one customer, "that I felt like I was sitting at Granny's table." Actually, this full-flavored, voluptuous dish is particularly popular with all our customers. We warn you, however, that the cabbage needs lengthy cooking, so start this dish early in the afternoon. For the noodles, use any dried ones you like, cook according to package directions, and serve with butter.

7 to 8 pounds cabbage
1 large onion, chopped
2 cloves garlic, minced
2 tablespoons sweet
  butter, melted
5 pounds ground beef
¼ cup chopped fresh
  parsley
2 teaspoons kosher salt
1 teaspoon ground black
  pepper
½ cup bread crumbs
2 large eggs

2 sixteen-ounce packages
  medium egg noodles

SAUCE

10 stalks celery, chopped
3 large onions, thinly sliced
½ cup vegetable oil
1 cup red wine
2 tablespoons kosher salt
2 teaspoons ground white pepper
2¼ cups firmly packed brown sugar
1 cup black raisins
¼ cup freshly squeezed lemon
  juice (from about 3 lemons)
2 tablespoons tomato paste
3 cups canned plum tomatoes
  with liquid
½ cup chopped fresh parsley
3 cups beef stock

Place whole cabbage or cabbages in a large pot with water to cover. Cook over medium heat for 15 to 20 minutes (longer for larger cabbages) until leaves are soft but still firm. Remove cabbage from pot, drain, and set aside to cool. You may have to remove outer leaves and return cabbage to pot to cook inside leaves.

Sauté onion and garlic in butter until soft. In a large bowl, combine onion and garlic with meat, parsley, salt, pepper, bread crumbs and eggs.

When cabbage is cool enough to handle, cut out core and remove leaves, keeping them whole by cutting against the core and prying leaves away one by one. Place 2 tablespoons of meat mixture on each leaf near the base. Fold cabbage over meat, fold in sides, and roll up tightly. Set stuffed leaves aside, folded side down.

To make sauce, sauté chopped celery and sliced onions in the oil in a large pot. Add the wine, raise heat, and reduce liquid by half. Stir remaining ingredients into the sauce. Add stuffed cabbage leaves. Simmer 2 to 2½ hours.

Preheat oven to 375 degrees. Remove stuffed leaves from sauce and place them in an 18-by-12-inch baking pan. Cover cabbage rolls with sauce and bake 20 minutes, or until tops begin to brown.

While cabbage rolls are baking, cook noodles according to package directions. Remove from water, drain, and toss with butter.

To serve, place cabbage rolls on top of noodles. Spoon sauce over both.

ROAST LEG OF LAMB

with

MUSTARD CASSIS CRUST

..

STRING BEANS

with

FENNEL

..

SWEET POTATO PANCAKES

..

ROASTED RED PEPPERS

SERVES This makes a wonderful Sunday supper for company. For those cooks who are intimidated by a
_____8_____ leg of lamb, our recipe is simple with dramatic
results. It combines several tastes we love with meat—garlic,
mustard and, for sweetness, cassis. The mustard-cassis paste
cuts lamb's natural fatty taste while it seals in the juices.

We discovered the string bean recipe by accident. We love
crunchy beans, and know that steamed beans need watching
or they can easily become soft. We decided to roast our beans
instead. This keeps their wonderful texture, enhances their
flavor and camouflages any imperfect beans. Roasted beans
do spoil quickly, however, so they can't be used as leftovers
in the next day's salad.

The sweet potato pancakes are a Jewish-American-style dish which we concocted.

For a final accent, decorate each serving with sliced roasted red peppers. These are typically Provençal, and make a beautiful garnish.

We use mustard often and in many guises: in salad dressings, to spark leftovers, to spread on sandwiches. So we keep three different kinds on hand: dry mustard, ideal to use when sautéing because prepared mustards turn bitter; regular French mustard; and grainy Dijon mustards. Inexpensive commercial types are too sweet for our taste.

ROAST LEG OF LAMB

SERVES
8

  1   cup cassis liqueur
  3   medium cloves garlic, minced
 ¼   cup olive oil
 ½   cup Dijon or other coarse-grain mustard
  1   teaspoon fresh thyme
  1   tablespoon ground white pepper
  2   teaspoons kosher salt
1¼   teaspoons paprika
 ¼   pound Parmesan cheese, grated, or Brie, julienned
6½   pound leg of lamb, boned and tied
  1   cup red wine
  3   ribs celery, cleaned

Preheat oven to 350 degrees.

Pour the cassis into a small saucepan, and reduce to ¼ cup over medium high heat, about 8 to 10 minutes.

Meanwhile, combine the garlic, mustard and spices in the container of a food processor. With the machine running, slowly pour in the cassis, olive oil, and Parmesan cheese. (If you are not using a food processor, combine all these ingredients in a small mixing bowl, and beat together with a wire whisk.) Spread the paste evenly over the lamb. (If using sliced Brie instead of Parmesan, layer the cheese over the mustard paste on the lamb half an hour before it finishes roasting.)

Pour the wine into roasting pan. Then, lay the celery on the bottom to form a bed for the lamb and place the lamb on top. Place the roasting pan in the oven and cook for 1¼ to 1½ hours. The meat will be medium rare.

STRING BEANS WITH FENNEL

SERVES
8

2½ pounds green beans
 1 tablespoon fennel seeds
 2 teaspoons kosher salt
¼ cup plus 1 tablespoon olive oil

Rinse the beans well, then pile them in front of you on a work surface. Snap off the "strings," or narrow side of the beans with your fingers—never use a paring knife or the beans will oxidize. Discard the strings, then put the beans into a mixing bowl. Add the fennel seeds, salt, and olive oil, mixing well so the beans are coated with oil. To keep from saturating the beans with oil, let the excess oil drip off after tossing, then lay the beans on a cookie sheet. Place in a 350-degree oven and roast for 15 to 20 minutes, until edges become brown.

Because of its uniform grains, crushed pepper is best for cooking; peppercorns, for grinding at the table. White pepper goes in our light sauces but has more kick than black.

SWEET POTATO PANCAKES

SERVES
8

4 large sweet potatoes, washed, dried, unpeeled
    and grated on large side of grater
2 Granny Smith apples, peeled, cored and grated
    on large side of grater
1 large Spanish onion, chopped
3 extra large eggs
2 teaspoons black pepper
2 teaspoons kosher salt
4 large cloves garlic, chopped
2 large eggs
8 tablespoons all-purpose flour
    pinch of red pepper flakes
    vegetable oil for frying

Combine all the ingredients except the oil in a large mixing bowl. Add the oil to the skillet for frying and heat the oil to 375 degrees.

Using a ¼ cup-size measuring cup, scoop up the batter and pat it gently until it holds together. With a spoon, put the batter into the skillet. You can fry up to 8 pancakes at once, depending on skillet size, but take care not to overcrowd the skillet. Fry each 3 to 5 minutes per side, or until both sides are golden. Remove from the skillet and drain them briefly on paper toweling before serving.

ROASTED RED PEPPERS

5 large red peppers
 olive oil
 fresh or dried *herbes de provençe*, to taste (see glossary)

Lay each pepper on a burner of your stove, and over high flame or heat, roast them turning them with a long-handled fork or tongs, until the skin blackens and the flesh becomes tender, but not mushy.

Remove the peppers from the heat and allow them to cool for about 15 minutes in a brown paper bag. Remove from bag, peel off the burned skin, and remove and discard the core and seeds. Slice the peppers into ½-inch-thick pieces, and put them into a mixing bowl. Add olive oil to cover and the herbs.

Roasted vegetables are particularly delicious. Whichever vegetable you select for roasting, from garlic to Brussels sprouts, coat with olive oil and sprinkle with kosher salt. To prevent the vegetables from being oversaturated with oil, toss everything together in a large stainless steel bowl, and let the oil drip off the vegetables as you remove them from the bowl. Then, spread the vegetables in a roasting pan or a cookie sheet, and put in a medium oven. Roast until tender.

MEATLOAF
with
SPICY MUSHROOM GRAVY

..

MASHED POTATOES

..

DILLED PEAS AND CARROTS

SERVES   When we crave a hearty meal, we think of this
8   meatloaf with all its trimmings—the ultimate in
         home-style dinners.

Discard the notion that you can't serve meatloaf to company. This particular meatloaf is so delectable that Carrie served it at her wedding. For best results, follow our recipe exactly, using our meat ratios for the proper balance of fat to lean. Also, never overhandle the meat, or the meatloaf will have a bready, flat, cottony taste. For easiest and best mixing, the meat should be at room temperature and added last to the other ingredients. Canned tomato soup provides a wonderful creamy taste; if you are a purist, you can replace the soup with heavy cream and chunked tomatoes. Meatloaf lends itself to leftover additions, and after you have become familiar with the taste of this recipe, you can experiment with your own additions. After her wedding, Carrie had to use up mountains of meatloaf meat. For the next two weeks, she served it with corn, with cheese and sour cream, with roasted red peppers and fried onions, and just plain with ketchup.

Whether or not you like lumpy mashed potatoes is a matter of personal taste. We happen to like ours light and fluffy, perhaps with a few lumps, so we slightly overcook the potatoes, a trick Carrie learned from Chef Seppi Renggli of The Four Seasons Restaurant in New York. Follow directions for cooking potatoes, highlighted on page 77, then mash them according to the following recipe. When you serve these, make a well in the center of the potatoes, and dribble meat pan juices into the well. This gives a really homemade look.

With the peas, we use fresh carrots cut into rounds. If you prefer, cut them into any shape you wish, but remember to account for the change in cooking time.

MEATLOAF

S E R V E S
8

4	tablespoons sweet butter or bacon fat
2	large onions, chopped
2	large cloves garlic, minced
3	celery stalks, sliced
2	medium-sized green bell peppers, diced
1	quart mushrooms, sliced
2	teaspoons kosher salt
1½	teaspoons black pepper
½	teaspoon paprika
¾	cup ketchup
1	tablespoon mayonnaise
2	teaspoons Worcestershire sauce
1	can cream of tomato or cream of mushroom soup, or ½ cup heavy cream
1	tablespoon tomato paste
2	medium eggs
¼	cup grated Parmesan cheese
1½	teaspoons dried basil, crushed
1½	teaspoons dried oregano, crushed
¼	cup chopped fresh parsley
1¼	cups plain bread crumbs
2	pounds ground chuck combined with 1 pound ground veal and 1 pound ground pork, at room temperature
6	slices bacon
	Spicy Mushroom Gravy (recipe follows)

Preheat the oven to 400 degrees.

Melt the butter or bacon fat in a skillet; add the onions, garlic, celery, bell peppers, mushrooms and salt and pepper. Sauté 10 minutes without browning. Remove from heat and allow to cool.

In a large mixing bowl, combine cooled vegetables and remaining ingredients for meatloaf except ground meat and bacon. Add the ground meat, blending well with both hands. Do not overwork or meatloaf will be mealy.

Divide the mixture in half, shaping each half into a 10-by-5-inch loaf. Lay bacon strips on top. Set loaves in roasting pan and bake 15 minutes. Turn temperature down to 350 degrees and bake 40 to 50 minutes longer. Remove loaves from oven and allow to set 10 to 15 minutes before cutting. Serve with Spicy Mushroom Gravy.

SPICY MUSHROOM GRAVY

YIELDS 4 CUPS

¼ cup sweet butter
¼ cup vegetable oil
1 bunch scallions, cut lengthwise into thin slices
3 large cloves garlic, minced
   large green bell pepper, cut in ¼-inch dice
1½ teaspoons salt
1 teaspoon ground white pepper
1 teaspoon ground black pepper
¼ teaspoon cayenne
1 teaspoon paprika
½ teaspoon dry mustard
½ cup plus 1 tablespoon meatloaf drippings
¼ cup plus 2 tablespoons all-purpose flour
1 cup red wine
2 teaspoons tomato paste
3½ cups beef stock
1 pound mushrooms, sliced
   beurre manié (see glossary) made with 2 tablespoons all-purpose flour plus 2 tablespoons sweet butter, softened (optional)

(continued on next page)

Heat butter and oil in a medium saucepan; add vegetables and spices and cook 5 to 7 minutes over medium heat, stirring constantly. After the meatloaf has cooked for 30 minutes, there should be enough drippings for the gravy, so add ½ cup meatloaf drippings. Stir in flour, scraping bottom of saucepan and stirring; cook 10 to 12 minutes, until roux is dark. Add wine and reduce liquid by half. Stir in tomato paste and 3 cups stock.

In a small skillet, sauté mushrooms in 1 tablespoon drippings over medium heat for 5 minutes. Raise heat and add remaining stock. Transfer to vegetable mixture in saucepan. Simmer, stirring, 10 minutes. Whisk in *beurre manié*, if needed, to thicken gravy to desired consistency.

We love handling our foods throughout every stage of shopping, preparation and serving. Despite some people's qualms, food handling is neither upsetting nor unsanitary. To the contrary, serious cooks find that hands-on food preparation is the best way to keep track of textures and consistencies, to feel what is actually happening to food and to prevent mistakes.

MASHED POTATOES

SERVES
8

     5 to 6 pounds Idaho potatoes
    ½ cup warm milk
     4 tablespoons butter, cut up
     2 teaspoons kosher salt
    ½ teaspoon ground white pepper
        pinch of nutmeg

Fill a large bowl with cold water and a pinch of salt. Cutting out blemishes first, peel potatoes. Cut the potatoes evenly into eighths; as each potato is cut, place in the cold water.

When ready to cook, drain and place potatoes in a large pot or stockpot and cover with fresh water with salt. Bring to a boil, lower heat, and simmer potatoes 20 to 30 minutes, or until very tender when pierced with a fork.

Drain potatoes and rinse with warm water to remove the starch. Drain again. Return potatoes to cooking pot, and allow to cool for only 5 minutes, or they will become sticky. Mash potatoes. When mashed, push potatoes to one side of the pot. Dent the potatoes in several places with a spoon handle to allow steam to escape (this helps to lighten the potatoes). Add milk, butter, salt, pepper and nutmeg to the empty half of pot. Place pot over medium heat until butter is melted and milk is scalding. Remove pot from heat and stir all ingredients vigorously to combine.

To scald milk, heat it until tiny bubbles appear around the edge of the milk where it touches the saucepan. But do not let the milk boil.

We were told by Chef Seppi Renggli in New York City that the best way to sharpen a potato peeler is—to peel potatoes.

We always use large Idahos for baking and mashing. They have the best flavor, texture and color. Before peeling them, rinse them off, then cut out any black spots. To peel, rest one end of the potato on the table and scrape off the potato skin away from you. Then slice off both ends. Cube each potato into about 8 pieces.

DILLED PEAS AND CARROTS

SERVES
8

2 pounds carrots, cut in ⅛-inch circles
   a few drops plus 1 teaspoon lemon juice
   16-ounce package frozen young peas, thawed
3 tablespoons chopped fresh dill
2 tablespoons sweet butter
   kosher salt to taste
   ground black pepper to taste

(continued on next page)

Blanch the carrots in water with a few drops of lemon juice following the directions highlighted on page 64. Drain. In a mixing bowl,
toss carrots with the peas and dill.

Just before serving, melt butter and add salt, pepper, the teaspoon of lemon juice and the vegetables. Sauté over medium heat
until heated through.

*Cutting carrots is a similar skill to cutting zucchini.
Place the carrot on a cutting board, with the root end
pointing toward you. With a vegetable peeler, make
quick, clean strokes away from you to scrape off the
surface from the bottom half of the carrot. Turn it as you
scrape. Make sure you end up with a perfectly smooth
and rounded carrot, and that you do not miss cleaning
any spots. After you have scraped all around, scrape the
root half. Like zucchini, carrots can be cut into different
shapes to suit different recipes. Chunks: Cut on the diagonal, as with zucchini. Julienne: Cut off the stem and
root ends, then slice the carrot into 2 or 3 chunks. Stand
each chunk on its end, and square it off with even,
straight cuts. Stack up the squared pieces, and cut
through them to make matchstick slices.*

BARBECUED PORK CHOPS

..

BAKED SWEET AND IDAHO POTATO CHIPS

..

LEMON-PARMESAN ZUCCHINI

SERVES If you love old-fashioned cookouts and foods
coated with thick, dribbly barbecue sauce, you'll
_____8_____ love this pork dish. It will remind you of all the
good flavors and good times of summer. If possible, make the
barbecue sauce a day in advance. It keeps well and tastes
better as it mellows. Our sauce recipe makes a lot, so you can
use with many different foods.

The dual-colored oven-baked potato chips are easy and,
unlike deep-fried chips, are not messy to cook. We leave the
skins on for extra vitamins.

The zucchini is a spunky dish and is delicious with poultry
and beef too.

BARBECUED PORK CHOPS

SERVES
8

16 pork chops at least ½ inch thick
2 cups Barbecue Sauce (recipe follows)

Preheat the oven to 375 degrees.

Arrange the chops on the baking sheet. Cover them with the barbecue sauce, making sure they are well coated. Bake only 30 to 40 minutes; do not overcook. If desired, chops can be cooked on top of the stove (in a frying pan, at 7 to 9 minutes a side) instead of in the oven.

BARBECUE SAUCE
FOR PORK

MAKES
ABOUT
7 CUPS

2 large onions, chopped
4 cloves garlic, minced
½ cup vegetable oil
1½ teaspoons kosher salt
1 tablespoon ground
   black pepper
¼ teaspoon cayenne
1 tablespoon paprika
4 tablespoons wine vinegar
5¼ cups ketchup (42 ounces)
1 cup firmly packed brown sugar

4 tablespoons tomato paste
¼ cup apricot jam
2 tablespoons hot pepper
   sauce
1 tablespoon
   Worcestershire sauce
1 cup soy sauce
½ cup honey
1 tablespoon lemon juice
2 tablespoons Dijon
   mustard

Sweat the onions and garlic in the oil over medium heat until slightly softened, about 5 minutes. Make sure garlic does not burn. Add the salt, pepper, cayenne and paprika and continue to cook, stirring occasionally, for 10 minutes. Add vinegar. Cook on medium heat for about 10 minutes, until almost all the liquid is completely evaporated. Add the remaining ingredients, stirring well up from the bottom. Turn heat to low, cover pot, and simmer for 1 hour, stirring frequently.

BAKED SWEET AND IDAHO POTATO CHIPS

**SERVES
8 OR MORE**

½ cup olive oil
2 teaspoons kosher salt
1½ teaspoons dried thyme, crushed
½ teaspoon ground ginger
2 pounds Idaho potatoes
2 pounds sweet potatoes

thyme

Line baking sheets with parchment paper. Preheat oven to 375 degrees. Combine the oil, salt, thyme and ginger in a large bowl; set aside.

Wash and dry all the potatoes. Without peeling the vitamin-packed skins, but removing any blemishes, slice Idaho potatoes into ¼-inch-thick circles, placing them in the oil mixture and stirring to coat them well. If desired, potatoes can be sliced in advance and placed in a bowl. Slice cleaned and unpeeled sweet potatoes into ½-inch-thick circles and also coat them well with the oil mixture.

Place the potatoes on the prepared baking sheets in a single layer and roast 20 to 25 minutes, until lightly browned. Serve immediately.

LEMON-PARMESAN ZUCCHINI

**SERVES
8**

4 tablespoons sweet butter
2 teaspoons kosher salt
1 teaspoon ground white pepper
½ teaspoon ground black pepper
4 large zucchini, seeded and cut into julienne
½ cup grated Parmesan cheese
juice of 1 lemon
2 lemons cut into wedges

Heat butter with the salt and the peppers over medium heat until it sizzles. Add the zucchini and sauté, stirring, 2 minutes. Add the

Parmesan and stir until zucchini are golden brown. Place the zucchini on warmed plates.

Add lemon juice to the pan to deglaze, stirring up brown bits from the bottom of the skillet. Pour pan juices over the zucchini.

Place pork chops and potatoes on plate with zucchini and garnish with lemon wedges.

We dislike serving a lukewarm meal, so we serve up our entrees on heated dinner plates—never so hot, of course, that they overcook the meal or burn hands. The best way to warm up plates is to place them in a barely warm oven for just a few moments before serving time. Of course, if you are preparing oven-cooked food or if your plates cannot withstand oven temperatures, you can't do this. Instead, run the plates under hot tap water for a minute or two and dry immediately.

SWEET-AND-
SOUR RIBS

..

DEEP-FRIED
NEW POTATOES

..

SAUTÉED KALE

..

FRUIT COMPOTE
TRIPLE SEC

SERVES For these ribs, coated in a sweet-and-pungent
sauce, use baby back or spare ribs. Unlike most
6 TO 8 pork dishes, this tastes lean and crunchy, not
fatty.

We take deep-frying potatoes seriously, and have found
that to achieve the perfect texture—crunchy outside, soft
inside—the potatoes must partially cook in water first, then
finish by frying in hot oil till golden brown. The red skins
remain and add a splash of color.

Carrie learned the technique for cooking kale when she
worked in a Manhattan restaurant for several months, where
this was so popular that she sautéed pounds of kale every
night. It is delicious.

If you decide to accompany this meal with the compote,
remember to make it a day in advance so that the flavors have
a chance to blend. Remove it from the refrigerator at least
2 hours in advance.

SWEET-AND-SOUR RIBS

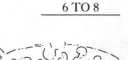

½ cup soy sauce
1 teaspoon paprika
1 teaspoon kosher salt
1 teaspoon ground white pepper
½ teaspoon cayenne
1 tablespoon chopped garlic
¼ cup wine vinegar or rice vinegar
1 tablespoon freshly squeezed lemon juice
⅔ cup firmly packed brown sugar
3 whole cloves
¼ cup maple syrup
1 tablespoon ground ginger
2 cups apricot jam
6 pounds spare ribs, cut into single bone servings
2 eleven-ounce cans mandarin oranges, drained

Preheat oven to 400 degrees.

Combine all ingredients except spare ribs and oranges in a medium saucepan and cook over low heat, stirring constantly until the sugar is dissolved. Raise heat to a slow boil and simmer the sauce about 20 minutes, or until it becomes slightly sticky.

Place ribs on a baking sheet so they do not overlap. Stir the oranges into the marinade, then pour it over the ribs, coating them well. (If time allows, marinate ribs, turning occasionally, 1 to 2 hours.)

Bake ribs for 10 minutes. Baste the ribs, and reduce the temperature to 350 degrees. Bake about 30 minutes; for more well done, crustier ribs, bake them about 45 minutes.

DEEP-FRIED NEW POTATOES

4 pounds uniform-sized new potatoes, unpeeled, parboiled, dried and quartered
vegetable oil for deep frying
kosher salt to taste

Fill fryer ⅔ full with oil. Preheat the oil to 330 to 350 degrees, or until a bread crumb turns golden in a few seconds. Line a large bowl with paper towels.

Carefully place several pieces of potato at a time into the oil. Cook 7 to 8 minutes, until golden. Remove to lined bowl with slotted spoon. Sprinkle with salt to taste. Repeat with remaining potatoes and salt.

Deep-frying is a wonderful way to change the taste and texture of food. A lot of people are frightened by this particular cooking technique, but if you are careful, you won't run into trouble. Follow these steps: Keep foods dry to prevent splattering in hot oil. Coat the food to protect it. Do not overheat the oil. Do not overload the deep-fryer. Do not overstir the batters so the gluten in the flour does not stiffen. A good way to test that the oil is the proper temperature is to drop a cube of bread into it. If it rises to the top and cooks to golden brown, the oil is fine. Play with the temperature control to find the proper setting for what you want to cook, depending on the equipment you have. Use long-handled tongs or slotted spoon to place ingredients into oil and remove them from it. The longer-handled your utensil is, the more protection you give your hands and arms from burns. If oil pops when you add the food, something is wet. Stop and check it out. Keep a plate or basket nearby, lined with paper towels, for draining just-fried foods.

Use a vegetable oil or shortening; never use butter because it burns too quickly and at a much lower temperature than oil. You can reuse the oil by cleaning it. Strain the oil through several layers of paper towels that line a sieve.

Kale, the spinachlike vegetable, has become very popular recently. It is sturdy, and the leaves don't shrink as much as spinach does. To prepare kale, snap off the stem of each stalk at the base of the leaf. Peel the tough central vein off each leaf with your fingers. Then rip each leaf into 3 or 4 sections. Do not use a knife—cutting changes the texture.

SAUTÉED KALE

SERVES
6 TO 8

- 1 cup vegetable oil, or ½ cup bacon fat or duck fat
- 2 large bunches kale (stems removed), washed and thoroughly dried
- 1 tablespoon kosher salt
- 1½ tablespoons lemon juice

Heat ½ to ⅓ of the oil or fat in a skillet. Add a couple of pinches of salt and half the lemon juice. The lemon juice will splatter, but it will evaporate and leave its flavor.

Place ⅓ of the kale leaves in the oil and push down with slotted spoon a few times. Cook 1½ minutes, then turn leaves over. Cook 1 to 2 minutes on the second side, pushing down frequently with the spoon. Remove from pan with tongs. Repeat the same procedure with rest of kale and oil or fat.

FRUIT COMPOTE TRIPLE SEC

MAKES
4 TO 5 CUPS

- ¼ cup freshly squeezed lemon juice
- ¼ cup Triple Sec
- 3 apples
- 2 pears
- 2 oranges
- 1 pint strawberries, hulled and halved
- 3 whole cloves
- ½ teaspoon ground cinnamon
- ¼ teaspoon ground black pepper
- 1 tablespoon sugar

Combine the lemon juice and Triple Sec over medium heat and reduce by half. Remove from heat.

Peel, core and cut apples into 1-inch pieces. Stir into Triple Sec reduction. Repeat with pears.

Grate the zest of 1 orange into the pear-apple mixture; peel the remaining orange. Cut both oranges into sections following directions highlighted below (cut the wedges over the saucepan to catch the juice) and add to saucepan. Stir in the strawberries, spices and sugar, and cook over low heat until the fruit is soft but still retains its shape. This takes 20 to 25 minutes. Cool and serve at room temperature.

Oranges and lemons are versatile fruits, and can be used in many creative ways. When grating either fruit, remember that their thick peels consist of 3 layers, and you want only the colored top layer. The white layers below are very bitter. Using the small side of your grater, brush the surface of the fruit across it in short strokes. Keep turning the fruit. Let the grated peel fall into a small bowl; using a pastry brush, scrape off any peel from the inside of the grater.

To cut up these fruits for a salad, slice off the ends, then lay one end flat on a level surface. With a sawing motion from top to bottom, slice off all skin and white pith. You will be left with a perfectly round fruit. Hold it over a bowl to catch the juices, and then with a sharp paring knife, cut out the sections, leaving the tough segments.

For garnishes, slice either fruit in half lengthwise, and then cut into ¼-inch crescents. For a colorful lemon garnish, dip one side of the crescent into chopped parsley, and the other side into paprika.

DEVILED SHORT RIBS

..

MASHED BUTTERNUT SQUASH

..

COLLARD GREENS

SERVES This is a great, beefy kind of meal. The ribs are very soft from long cooking, and the spicy sauce **8** has a tangy aftertaste. It's spicier than most meat sauces, because when we were creating it, we inadvertently added extra pepper, and we liked the results. The ribs are messy to eat, so don't serve them at a formal dinner party. We picked the side dishes for their zesty colors. We learned how to cook the collard greens from a former dishwasher of ours—a zany kid who wore shorts all year. All in all, a real down-home meal.

DEVILED SHORT RIBS

SERVES
8

- 8 pounds beef short ribs, separated
- 1½ cups all-purpose flour combined with 1 teaspoon salt and ½ teaspoon pepper
- ⅔ cup vegetable oil
- 1 large onion, chopped
- 2 cloves garlic, minced
- ½ cup red wine
- 1½ cups ketchup
- 1 tablespoon hot pepper sauce
- 1 teaspoon cayenne
- 2 teaspoons Worcestershire sauce
- 2 teaspoons salt
- 1 teaspoon ground black pepper
- ½ teaspoon dried thyme
- 1 tablespoon tomato paste
- 2 tablespoons Dijon mustard
- 2 cups beef stock

thyme

Dredge ribs in seasoned flour. Preheat oil; add 5 or 6 ribs at a time and brown over medium heat, turning often to prevent burning. Place browned ribs in stockpot, and repeat with remaining ribs. Pour off all but 2 tablespoons fat and sauté onion and garlic until golden; add to meat. Deglaze skillet with wine and reduce by half; add liquid to stockpot.

Combine remaining ingredients and add to meat, stirring well. Simmer, uncovered, 2½ hours, stirring occasionally.

MASHED BUTTERNUT SQUASH

YIELDS
5 CUPS

- 3 large butternut squash (about 8 pounds) halved lengthwise and seeded
- 4 tablespoons sweet butter, softened
- 1½ teaspoons kosher salt
- ½ teaspoon ground white pepper
- ⅛ teaspoon ground nutmeg

(continued on next page)

Preheat oven to 350 degrees. Arrange squash cut side down on baking sheets. Bake 35 to 40 minutes, or until flesh is completely soft. Turn cut side up, and cool 15 minutes. Scoop out flesh of the squash into a saucepan and mash until smooth, making several wells to allow excess moisture to evaporate. Return to low heat and cook for 3 to 5 minutes, then stir in butter and spices until well blended.

COLLARD GREENS

SERVES
8

½ cup vegetable oil
1 large onion, chopped
2 large cloves garlic, minced
1 tablespoon ground white pepper
1 teaspoon cayenne
1 tablespoon brown sugar
1 ham hock
2 tablespoons vinegar
4½ pounds collard greens, washed, trimmed and drained
2 tablespoons hot pepper sauce

Preheat oil. Sauté onion with garlic, white pepper, cayenne and sugar. Add ham hock and cook 10 minutes. Stir in vinegar; reduce by half. Add greens, stir to coat well, then add hot pepper sauce and 2 cups water. Bring to a boil, reduce heat and simmer uncovered 1½ hours. Adjust seasonings. When ready, remove from heat. Remove meat from pot, cut away from bone and shred. Return meat to pot, stirring well. Reheat briefly. Serve when heated through.

SHEPHERD'S
PIE

and

PEA
SALAD

SERVES We are just wild about this English tavern food,
        popular at Good Enough to Eat with both kids
___8___ and adults. Our recipe varies from the traditional
one; ours is more peasanty, and we have layered all the ingredients, rather than mixing everything together. Also, since
we do not totally drain off the fat, ours tends to be very juicy.
One friend of ours said, "If I were food, I would like to be
your shepherd's pie." He eats with us every week, and when
we told him that we would serve shepherd's pie for him every
Wednesday night, he yelled to his girlfriend, "The angels are
singing, because we can eat shepherd's pie each week." He
orders, and eats, two full servings.

The pea salad—tart and cheesy—provides a taste and color
counterpoint and replaces the typical accompaniment of fat
green peas the British serve with their shepherd's pie. This
salad is one of our original recipes from the days when we
were a takeout place. It has always been a sellout dish. With
this meal, we suggest a mug or two of hard cider.

SHEPHERD'S PIE

Mashed potatoes from 5 pounds cooked Idaho potatoes

VEGETABLE MIXTURE

½ cup olive oil
2 onions, chopped
3 carrots, peeled and chopped
6 stalks celery, chopped finely
2 teaspoons kosher salt
2 teaspoons paprika
1 teaspoon white pepper
1½ teaspoons dried basil
1 bay leaf

MEAT MIXTURE

4 pounds ground beef
½ teaspoon cayenne pepper
1 teaspoon black pepper
1 teaspoon kosher salt
2 teaspoons tomato paste
2 tablespoons red wine
1 tablespoon Worcestershire sauce
1 bay leaf
2¼ cups ketchup

basil

TOPPING

½ cup grated Parmesan cheese
paprika for sprinkling

Preheat oven to 375 degrees.

Prepare mashed potatoes according to directions in the Meatloaf dinner (see page 112). Set aside.

For the Vegetable Mixture: Put the olive oil into a skillet over low heat, and add all the vegetables and spices. Sweat (see glossary) them for 15 minutes, or until translucent. Put the cooked vegetables into a large mixing bowl.

For the Meat Mixture: In the same skillet, put beef, pepper and salt and cook over medium heat. Use a large fork to separate the meat to remove any large clumps. After the meat starts to stick to the bottom of the skillet, add the tomato paste and wine to deglaze it. When the liquid has almost completely reduced, add the Worcestershire sauce, bay leaf, and ketchup. Cook for another 15 or 20 minutes, or until the meat is slightly browned.

To assemble the pie, put the meat into a large baking dish, skimming off excess fat until only a thin layer remains. Spread out the meat evenly, then top with the vegetable mixture. Spread the mashed potatoes over top, making striations on the surface with a fork. Sprinkle with Parmesan cheese and paprika. Bake for 15 minutes at 375 degrees, then reduce the heat to 325 degrees, and cook for another 20 minutes.

PEA SALAD

SERVES

8

  1 cup mayonnaise
  1 tablespoon Dijon mustard
 ¼ cup olive oil
  1 teaspoon lemon juice
1½ teaspoons kosher salt
 ½ teaspoon ground white pepper
 ½ teaspoon paprika
2½ pounds frozen young peas, thawed and drained, cooked as directed on box
  1 medium-sized red onion, chopped
 ½ pound Cheddar cheese, grated

Whisk together mayonnaise, mustard, oil, lemon juice, salt, pepper and paprika.

Combine peas, onion and cheese. Stir in mayonnaise mixture gently just until vegetables are coated.

Serve at room temperature.

BEEF STEW

This chunky meal—a great winter's dinner—needs no accompaniment other than a beverage and hot bread. We suggest using a commercial condensed tomato sauce in the stew for a more intense tomato taste; but, conversely, we urge you to use a homemade beef stock. Canned stocks are too salty and give the stew a tinny taste hard to disguise. Use the leanest possible beef, so the stew won't be fatty. Follow the cooking sequence carefully so that the meat cooks until tender, but the vegetables do not overcook.

   4 tablespoons sweet butter
   2 tablespoons olive oil
   2 teaspoons plus 1 tablespoon kosher salt
   2 teaspoons plus 1 tablespoon ground black pepper
   1 tablespoon brown sugar (if not using prunes, as listed below)
   3 medium onions, chopped
   4 medium cloves garlic, minced
   6 celery stalks, cut in 1-inch pieces
   1 cup vegetable oil
1½ cups all-purpose flour
   1 teaspoon paprika
   8 pounds stewing beef, trimmed and cut into 1½-inch cubes
      12-ounce bottle stout
  10 cups beef stock
   2 tablespoons tomato paste
   3 cups canned tomato sauce
   2 teaspoons dried thyme, crushed
   1 tablespoon dried basil, crushed
   3 bay leaves
   5 pounds carrots, peeled and sliced in 1-inch pieces
5½ pounds Idaho potatoes, peeled and cut in 1-inch cubes
  30 pitted prunes softened in ½ cup rum and ¼ cup hot water for 15 mintues; then drain and discard liquid (optional) or reduce liquid to 2 teaspoons
      beurre manié (optional) (see glossary)
  ½ cup chopped fresh parsley

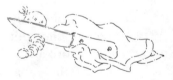

In Dutch oven or stockpot combine the butter, olive oil, 2 teaspoons each salt and pepper, and sugar (if using), over medium heat 2 minutes. Add the onions, garlic and celery, and cook 15 minutes, stirring frequently. Remove vegetables and set aside. Add the cup of vegetable oil to pot.

Combine the flour with the paprika and 1 tablespoon each salt and pepper. Dredge beef in seasoned flour. Turn heat to medium high and place several pieces of meat at a time into the pot without crowding. Brown meat on all sides, about 10 minutes. Remove meat to bowl and brown remaining pieces.

Deglaze pot with the stout, scraping to remove brown bits from bottom of the pot. Reduce liquid by half, then return meat and vegetables to the pot. Add the stock, tomato paste, tomato sauce, thyme, basil and bay leaves. Bring to a boil, then lower heat to a simmer. Cook, uncovered, 1 hour, stirring often. Add the carrots, potatoes, and drained prunes, if using, and simmer 1½ hours.

When meat is tender, bring liquid to a boil and whisk in *beurre manié*, if needed, to thicken gravy to the consistency of a thick milkshake. Fifteen minutes before serving, remove bay leaves and stir in parsley.

Dredging meat, or covering its surface with a thin film of flour, bread crumbs, cornmeal or batter prior to cooking, helps form a crisp exterior surface that browns nicely. In addition, the coating prevents fat from splattering, and keeps the meat from burning. Dredge meats just prior to cooking or the coating will turn soggy. Make sure the meat surface is evenly and thoroughly coated, shaking off any excess coating—otherwise it will fall off into the cooking fat and dirty it.

If you are dredging meat in a batter or liquid, then in flour or crumbs, set up an assembly line of bowls, the first with the batter, and the second with the dry coating. This way you can use one hand for the wet mixture, and keep the other dry and clean for the flour mixture and then for putting the meat into the cooking pot.

Poultry Meals

SOUTHERN FRIED CHICKEN BREASTS

with

MEAT CHILI SAUCE

..

GUACAMOLE

..

TOMATO AND CORN SALAD

SERVES With this meal we paired the South with the Southwest. This came about one morning when **8** we had a large pot of leftover chili, slightly over-spiced, and we needed a bland foil for it. Chicken breasts—we thought—and the resulting entree is a taste sensation. Our chili recipe makes lots, so you'll have plenty left over—and it even tastes better the next day, or the next week! Make it at least a day in advance, if possible. The soft guacamole adds contrasting color and texture, and the cold salad is a delicious palate cleanser after all that heavy-duty food.

SOUTHERN FRIED CHICKEN BREASTS WITH MEAT CHILI SAUCE

CHICKEN BREASTS

    1 cup all-purpose flour
    ⅓ cup cornmeal
    1 teaspoon kosher salt
    1 teaspoon black pepper
    ½ teaspoon baking soda
    ⅛ cup chopped fresh parsley
    2 large eggs
    1 cup buttermilk
    ⅓ cup dark ale
    ½ cup vegetable oil and ½ cup shortening for frying
    8 chicken breasts, halved and boned
      Meat Chili Sauce (recipe on page 134)

If a recipe calls for buttermilk and you do not have any on hand, you can make a reasonable facsimile by combining 2 cups of milk with 1 tablespoon lemon juice and 2 tablespoons sour cream. Allow this to stand several minutes until it clobbers (forms clots).

In a large bowl, combine the flour, cornmeal, salt, pepper, baking soda, and parsley; set aside.

In a separate bowl, whisk the eggs with the buttermilk and ale; set aside. In the meantime, trim the chicken breasts of fat and gristle. Pat chicken dry.

Heat the oil and shortening in a large, deep saucepan over medium-high heat (350 degrees), or until a cube of bread dropped in the pan rises to the top and immediately turns golden. Line platter with paper towel.

Dip each breast in the egg mixture, then dredge in flour, shaking off excess. Set each breast on a plate until ready to deep-fry. This should be done just prior to cooking.

Add the chicken breasts to the hot oil one at a time with tongs, being careful not to crowd the saucepan. Deep-fry 1 side 4 minutes, then turn the chicken with tongs and fry 2 minutes on the other side. Remove chicken to paper-towel-lined plate. Repeat with remaining chicken breasts.

Place 2 pieces of chicken on each plate and spoon chili over the top. Spoon some guacamole on the side, and next to it a portion of salad on top of 1 leaf of red lettuce.

MEAT CHILI SAUCE

YIELDS
10 TO 12
CUPS

4 red onions, chopped
2 cloves garlic, minced
½ cup olive oil
½ cup sweet butter
6 green bell peppers, chopped
4 pounds ground beef
6 cups canned crushed tomatoes
½ cup ketchup
1 tablespoon tomato paste
3 tablespoons kosher salt
3 teaspoons white pepper
2 bay leaves
4 tablespoons sweet butter
2 tablespoons chili powder
1 teaspoon ground cumin
1 teaspoon paprika
1 teaspoon cayenne
2 tablespoons hot pepper sauce
¾ cup honey
3 fourteen-ounce cans drained red kidney beans

Sauté onions and garlic in oil and butter in a stockpot over medium heat 10 minutes. Add bell peppers and sauté 15 minutes longer. Remove vegetables from stockpot and reserve.

Place meat in stockpot and brown and stir with a wooden spoon to break up lumps. Drain meat of fat and return to pot. Add tomatoes, ketchup, tomato paste, salt, 2 teaspoons white pepper and the bay leaves.

Melt the 4 tablespoons of butter in a skillet and sauté the chili powder, cumin, paprika, cayenne and 1 teaspoon pepper until cooked through. Add them to the meat mixture, stirring well. Add the onion and garlic mixture. Simmer, covered, 40 to 45 minutes. Add hot pepper sauce and honey and cook, uncovered, 30 minutes longer. Stir in the beans and cook 10 minutes more.

Incidentally, always sauté spices first in clarified butter to rid them of their bitter taste before adding them to any recipe for further cooking. On the other hand, herbs should never be sautéed.

GUACAMOLE

**MAKES
2¼ CUPS**

- 2 plum tomatoes
- 2 cloves garlic, chopped
- 1 teaspoon chopped fresh coriander
- ½ teaspoon kosher salt
- 1 teaspoon black pepper
- ⅛ teaspoon cayenne
- 2 drops hot pepper sauce
- 2 teaspoons freshly squeezed lime juice, or 1 tablespoon freshly squeezed lemon juice
- 2 ripe avocados

To peel tomatoes, core each tomato, cut a cross in the bottom. Dip into boiling water 8 seconds, then remove with a slotted spoon. Cool, then slip off the peel. Cut in half, then gently squeeze the tomato halves to remove the seeds. Chop tomatoes finely.

If using food processor, place garlic, coriander, salt, pepper, and cayenne, hot pepper sauce and lime or lemon juice in bowl and process until combined. Peel, pit and add the avocado and tomato and process until just combined.

If making guacamole by hand, grind garlic with salt and pepper using a mortar and pestle. Peel, pit, and mash the avocado, then gradually mash in remaining ingredients. Again, it's best to place avocado pit in guacamole to prevent the guacamole from browning.

Let sit at room temperature for ½ hour before serving.

TOMATO AND CORN SALAD

SERVES
8

16   plum tomatoes, cored and sliced in eighths
1½ cups drained canned corn kernels
  1   large clove garlic, chopped
  1   large red onion, thinly sliced
  1   tablespoon chopped fresh coriander
  1   tablespoon kosher salt
  1   teaspoon black pepper
       juice of 1 lemon or 2 limes
  1   cup vegetable oil
  2   to 3 drops hot pepper sauce
       red-leaf lettuce leaves for garnish

Combine all ingredients. Refrigerate, covered, at least 4 hours.

GLAZED RASPBERRY DUCK

with

LEMON SAUCE

and

GREEN AND PURPLE GRAPES

..

DIRTY RICE

..

ROAST BRUSSELS SPROUTS

..

APPLE FRITTERS

SERVES
_____8_____ After the light foods of summer, this makes a festive meal rich with all the powerful tastes of fall. Because duck can be so greasy and heavy, we avoided putting it on our menu for a long time. But so many people asked for it that we came up with this technique, a cross between the methods that both we and the chefs at The Four Seasons restaurant use to roast duck. The result

is a nongreasy bird. Actually, it is the epitome of our crunchy-mushy theory of food — a crackly skin envelops juicy, tender meat. We offer half a duck per person, but you can serve a quarter duck if you prefer.

Roast Brussels sprouts, pungent on their own, actually do not interfere with the gamey taste of the duck. Regional Southern cooking inspired the other two side dishes: dirty rice, named because of the color imparted by the duck livers, is a popular Creole dish. The apple fritters resemble those Southern favorites *beignets,* or fried sweet dough.

GLAZED RASPBERRY DUCK WITH LEMON SAUCE AND GREEN AND PURPLE GRAPES

S E R V E S
8

MARINADE

- 1 cup soy sauce
- 1 slice lemon
- ½ cup rice wine or dry sherry
- 1 tablespoon honey
- 2 large cloves garlic, peeled
- 2 tea bags (Chinese tea if possible)

- 4 ducks, quartered, skins pricked with fork

Combine marinade ingredients in saucepan and simmer 15 to 20 minutes to combine. Cool.

Place ducks in roasting pan and cover with marinade. Refrigerate, turning occasionally, at least 3 hours, or overnight.

One hour before serving, remove ducks and marinade from roasting pan. Discard marinade. Invert a baking sheet in a roasting pan and arrange ducks skin side up on baking sheet. Preheat oven to 425 degrees. Brush ducks with Glaze (recipe below).

Roast ducks 15 minutes. Turn temperature down to 325 degrees and brush ducks with remaining glaze. Roast 55 minutes longer.

At regular intervals, remove excess fat from roasting pan with a baster.

If your oven has room for only one roaster, first cook the dark pieces according to recipe directions. Then remove the dark pieces, add the light pieces and cook for around 40 minutes. When ready to serve, coat with lemon sauce.

GLAZE FOR DUCK

MAKES ABOUT 1½ CUPS

¼ cup sweet liqueur (Triple Sec, cassis, brandy, etc.)
1 cup raspberry, strawberry or apricot jam
2 tablespoons sugar
2 teaspoons lemon juice
¼ cup water

In a small saucepan reduce liqueur by half over low heat. Add jam, sugar, lemon juice and ¼ cup water and continue cooking over low heat. Swirl pan but do not stir until sugar is dissolved. Simmer 10 to 12 minutes, adding water, if needed, to achieve a spreadable consistency.

LEMON SAUCE WITH GRAPES

MAKES 4 CUPS

2 tablespoons cornstarch
1 tablespoon water
2 cups chicken stock
1 cup sugar
1½ teaspoons salt
½ teaspoon white pepper
1 cup fresh lemon juice
grated rind of 2 lemons
¼ pound seedless green grapes, halved
¼ pound seedless red grapes, halved

In a small bowl, dissolve cornstarch in water and set aside. In a medium saucepan, combine stock, sugar, salt and pepper. On medium heat, stir until sugar dissolves. Add cornstarch and reduce heat to low. Cook for 5 to 6 minutes, stirring occasionally. Add lemon juice and rind. Continue cooking for 4 to 5 minutes until sauce has thickened. Remove from heat and add halved grapes. Sauce may be reheated on low heat.

DIRTY RICE

SERVES
8

livers and gizzards from 4 ducks
2 teaspoons kosher salt
2 teaspoons ground black pepper
¼ teaspoon cayenne
¼ teaspoon ground cumin
¼ teaspoon paprika
¼ teaspoon dry mustard
4 tablespoons vegetable oil
1 green bell pepper, chopped
1 medium-sized onion, chopped
2 cloves garlic, minced
3 cups long-grain rice
3 cups chicken stock
3 cups water
2 bay leaves

With a sharp knife, cut fat and gristle from livers and gizzards using a sawing motion. Discard fat and gristle. Coarsely chop livers and gizzards.

In a medium saucepan, sauté salt, pepper, cayenne, cumin, paprika, and mustard in oil for 3 minutes. Add bell pepper, onion and garlic; sweat 15 minutes. Add rice, gizzards, and livers and stir-fry 5 minutes longer. Turn up heat, add stock, 3 cups water and the bay leaves and bring to a boil. Reduce heat, stir, and barely simmer, covered, 15 minutes, or until almost all of the liquid has been absorbed. Turn off the heat and let rice sit, covered, 5 minutes. Remove cover and fluff up the rice. Remove bay leaves before serving.

ROAST BRUSSELS SPROUTS

SERVES
8

3 pounds fresh Brussels sprouts, trimmed, and bottoms cut with an X
4 tablespoons olive oil
1 tablespoon kosher salt
1 teaspoon lemon juice

Thoroughly combine all ingredients in large bowl. Toss Brussels sprouts to coat well. Place sprouts on baking sheet and roast with the ducks at 325 degrees for about 40 minutes, or until sprouts are crunchy.

Or, if tight for oven space, a good alternative is to blanch the sprouts in salted water 4 to 7 minutes or until just tender. Just before serving time, sauté them in a large skillet over high heat with the oil, salt and lemon juice for about 7 minutes, or until heated through.

APPLE FRITTERS

SERVES
8

vegetable oil for deep frying

2 to 3 firm apples, peeled, cored and sliced in ½-inch-thick circles
1 tablespoon salt
1 tablespoon sugar

BATTER
1¼ cups all-purpose flour
½ cup rolled oats
   pinch of salt
2 tablespoons sugar
3 eggs
⅔ cup apple cider
1 tablespoon sweet butter, melted

Preheat oil to 325 degrees, or until a bread cube dropped in oil turns golden and rises to the top. Line a bowl with paper towels.

To make batter, combine flour, oats, salt and sugar. Make a well in the mixture.

Separate eggs. Beat yolks until light, then pour into the well in the dry mixture. Add apple cider and melted butter and slowly combine, whisking until batter is free of lumps.

Beat whites until stiff but not dry. Fold a large spoonful of the whites into the batter, then fold in remaining whites. Cover with plastic wrap and refrigerate for at least an hour.

Place several apple slices at a time in the batter, then in hot fat. Fry 3 to 4 minutes, until golden on one side. Turn fritters and fry 3 to 4 minutes longer.

Place in paper-towel-lined bowl to drain. Sprinkle with salt and sugar. Repeat with remaining batter and apples.

MARYLAND CORNISH HENS

with

SAUTÉED BANANAS

..

CORN FRITTERS

..

COLE SLAW

with

APPLES

.. : .. : .. : ..

S E R V E S This meal is a take-off on a classic Maryland dinner of fried chicken and corn fritters. For a **8** slightly more elegant company meal, we have substituted game hens for the larger chickens. The whole dinner is a wonderful combination of old-fashioned tastes. Remember to make the cole slaw at least 2 hours in advance.

MARYLAND CORNISH HENS
SERVES
8

    vegetable oil for deep-frying, or half vegetable oil
    and half shortening
2 cups buttermilk
3 large eggs
2 cups all-purpose flour
2 cups crushed cornflakes
1 teaspoon kosher salt
1 teaspoon white pepper
2 teaspoons paprika
4 Cornish hens, halved, cleaned and patted dry
8 slices bacon

Fill a deep-fat fryer ⅔ full with oil and preheat oil to 350 degrees, or until a cube of bread added to the oil turns golden and rises to the top.

Preheat oven to 250 degrees.

Meanwhile, whisk buttermilk with eggs. In a separate bowl, combine the flour with cornflakes, salt, pepper and paprika. Dip hens in buttermilk mixture, then dredge in flour mixture. Place several halves of the hens in oil without crowding and deep-fry 15 minutes, until hens are golden. Remove hens and place skin side up on a baking sheet and cover each with 1 slice of bacon. Repeat with remaining hens and bacon. Bake hens 20 minutes.

Remove oil from heat and skim for use in Corn Fritter recipe on page 145.

SAUTÉED BANANAS
SERVES
8

8 bananas, halved lengthwise
1 cup brandy, rum or orange juice
½ cup all-purpose flour
⅓ cup brown sugar
    pinch of kosher salt
8 to 16 tablespoons sweet butter

Soak bananas in the brandy, rum or orange juice for 5 to 7 minutes.

In a separate bowl, combine flour with sugar and salt. Preheat skillet over medium heat. Add butter to skillet and dredge bananas in flour mixture. When butter starts to foam, add bananas to skillet and sauté about 2 minutes each side, until golden. Remove bananas to serving plate, and drain all but 1 tablespoon of the pan juices. Turn heat to medium high and deglaze skillet with ½ cup of the brandy, rum or orange juice marinade. Reduce sauce to 2 tablespoons, and pour over bananas.

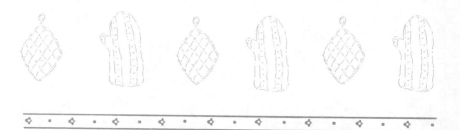

Chopping fresh parsley is a chore every cook must learn to do well. Here's our method. Rinse parsley sprigs well and pat them dry. Cut off all leafy heads and pile them into a mound, reserving the stems for flavoring stocks. With a chef's knife, first make big chops to reduce the parsley to smaller pieces. Keep pushing the pieces back into the mound as you chop. When the parsley bits are small, put both hands on the knife—one flat down on the top of the blade and the other on the handle—and, in a quick, rocking motion, mince the parsley fine.

Gather up the mound of chopped parsley, and wrap it in a cloth kitchen towel and squeeze. Run the bundle under cold water and wring it out well. This way, the flavor remains, but the strong-tasting parsley juices are washed away. Also, rinsed parsley lasts longer, and does not cling together.

CORN FRITTERS

SERVES
8

vegetable oil for deep-frying, or half vegetable oil
and half shortening (reserved from frying the Cornish hens)
1 cup all-purpose flour
2 teaspoons kosher salt
1 teaspoon black pepper
1 tablespoon baking powder
⅔ cup cornmeal
⅔ cup rolled oats
4 cups drained canned corn kernels
¼ cup chopped fresh parsley
¼ cup minced onion
½ teaspoon sugar dissolved in 1 cup flat beer
maple syrup

Preheat oil to 350 degrees, or until bread cube placed in oil turns golden and rises to the top. Line a large bowl with paper towels.

In a separate bowl, combine the flour with salt, pepper, baking powder, cornmeal and oats. Make a well in the center and add the corn, parsley and onion. As you start to stir, add the beer and combine thoroughly. Allow batter to rest 5 to 10 minutes.

Without crowding, drop batter by soupspoonfuls into oil and cook 2 to 3 minutes each side, until fritters are golden. (If the fritters start to turn grayish brown, lower the heat.)

Remove fritters to paper-towel-lined bowl to drain, and sprinkle with salt and pepper. Repeat with remaining batter. Serve 3 fritters on each plate, and pass maple syrup on the side.

COLE SLAW WITH APPLES

SERVES
8

¾ pound green cabbage, thinly shredded
¾ pound red cabbage, thinly shredded
½ pound carrots, peeled (after peeling off the outside, peel the rest into the bowl; you cannot peel the core)
3 Cortland or Granny Smith apples, peeled, cored and very thinly sliced
5 medium scallions, both white and green parts, very thinly sliced
1 green bell pepper, finely diced
1 red bell pepper, finely diced

DRESSING

2 teaspoons kosher salt
1½ teaspoons ground black pepper
⅛ teaspoon hot pepper sauce
½ cup Mayonnaise (page 63)
½ cup sour cream
1 tablespoon Dijon mustard
2 teaspoons lemon juice
2 tablespoons red wine vinegar
1 tablespoon caraway seeds
2 teaspoons maple syrup
⅓ cup olive oil combined with ⅓ cup melted bacon fat
4 to 5 large slices of bacon diced in ½-inch chunks, cooked

Combine salad vegetables in a large bowl. In a small bowl, place spices, mayonnaise, sour cream and mustard. Stir in lemon juice and vinegar, then caraway seeds and maple syrup.

Drizzle in the oil and fat, then sprinkle on bacon. It is better to mix the dressing on the side or the cabbage will bleed.

Add dressing and toss lightly. Then let cole slaw macerate in refrigerator for 30 minutes. Remove and let sit at room temperature for at least 1 hour before serving.

LEMON PARMESAN CHICKEN AND SHRIMP

..

FRESH PASTA

and

TOMATO CONCASSE

SERVES A light, refined company meal, this consists of
many complementary tastes—lemon, Parmesan
8 cheese, chicken and shrimp. It's an active meal,
which cooks very quickly and requires constant movement in
the final moments of preparation. So follow directions carefully to coordinate last-minute stove-top efforts. To be en-
ergy efficient, stand with your knees unlocked and arms loose
so your movements are fluid.

We prefer fresh pasta in any shape, usually fettuccine, but
if you cannot find it fresh, select a quality dried pasta instead.

The tomato concasse is very garlicky, but light. It adds
color and comes together quickly. We have added yellow
summer squash to this for an unusual variation. This is wonderful on rice or pasta, or mixed with chopped vegetables and
served on chicken or meat.

LEMON PARMESAN CHICKEN AND SHRIMP

SERVES
8

3 whole chicken breasts, skinned, boned and halved
18 large shrimp
½ cup all-purpose flour
½ cup grated Parmesan cheese
2 teaspoons kosher salt
1 teaspoon ground white pepper
½ teaspoon paprika
½ teaspoon dry mustard
4 large eggs, beaten
1 cup clarified sweet butter
¾ cup freshly squeezed lemon juice
   watercress for garnish
   Pasta and Tomato Concasse (recipe on page 150)

We always buy boned and skinless chicken breasts because they save precious preparation time. Breast meat is very tender and delicate, so treat it gently, as you would fish. It's a good idea to know how to bone a whole breast, in case that's all you have to work with. To trim a whole breast, lay it flat with its inside facing up. With your fingers, pull off the small tenderloins found on either side of the flat breast while holding the breast down with the knife. If you wish, cut out the white tendon, although this is not necessary. Set the tenderloins aside. To trim off fat from either side of the breast, scrape it off with the back of a knife and cut the fat away. Then slice out the central strip of gristle and bone. You will be left with two uniformly shaped breast pieces. Depending on the recipe, either use the breast piece as is, or cut each breast piece on the diagonal into thirds, or fourths.

   For some recipes you will need to pound the cleaned

and trimmed breasts flat. Place each piece between sheets of wax paper and, using a meat pounder or rolling pin, tap the meat flat gently with a pushing out motion, moving in all directions. Keep turning the breasts as you pound.

Trim chicken breasts. Remove the tenderloin and cut each half into 4 even pieces. Pat dry. Peel and devein the shrimp. Pat dry.

Combine the flour, cheese, salt, pepper, paprika and mustard. Place chicken and shrimp pieces in beaten eggs to coat, then dredge in the flour mixture.

Place half of butter in the skillet over medium heat. Heat until sizzling. Add half the chicken and half the shrimp, sauté 2 minutes on each side, until golden. Remove from skillet and keep warm. Repeat with remaining butter, chicken and shrimp.

Drain all but 4 tablespoons of the butter. Add the lemon juice and deglaze the pan, scraping bits from the bottom. Pour pan juices over shrimp and chicken before serving.

Place some pasta on a plate; top with tomato concasse and sprinkle with Parmesan cheese.

Arrange the chicken and shrimp on the other side of the plate. Garnish with watercress.

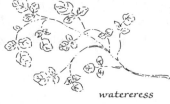

watercress

Watercress, a slightly tart, peppery-tasting green, is ideal for salads or as a garnish because it looks like a bouquet. For either use, snap off the woody stems just below the leaves. Stand the trimmed watercress clump head down in ice water until ready to use.

FRESH PASTA AND TOMATO CONCASSE

6 beefsteak tomatoes, cored, peeled and sliced in eighths, seeds removed
3 large cloves garlic, minced
¼ cup olive oil
2 teaspoons kosher salt
1 teaspoon ground black pepper
¼ cup chopped fresh basil, or 1 teaspoon dried and crushed

½ cup grated Parmesan cheese
2 pounds pasta, fresh if possible

Peel tomatoes by making a cross with a knife on the bottoms and plunging them into boiling water. Remove after 8 seconds, cool and peel.

For the pasta: Boil water in a large pot with a pinch of salt and 2 tablespoons oil. When boiling, add pasta. Cook until tender (the fresh will take a very few minutes, the dried a little longer) and drain.

In another pot, combine all ingredients except basil and cheese and simmer 7 minutes. Add basil and cook 10 minutes longer. The tomatoes should be soft but still retain their shape. Serve grated Parmesan on the side.

This dish can be prepared in advance (except the pasta) and reheated.

CHICKEN POT PIE

**SERVES
8 TO 10**

This traditional home-cooked meal reminds us of child-hood farm dinners. Everything is here—meat, vegeta-bles, crust and cheese. Ann remembers a similar pot pie served at a chicken farm in New Hampshire that had coops out back behind a white clapboard house. To Sunday guests the owners served chicken pot pies family style on an old wooden table.

A major complaint about most chicken pot pies is that they are dried out, heavy and soggy. We prevent that by using moist boneless poached breasts, and by adding extra liquid to the cream sauce. We sprinkle Cheddar cheese over the filling to keep the sauce from soaking into the crust and to give the creamy filling a distinctive rich taste. Besides the suggested vegetables, you can add any leftovers on hand—and leftover turkey makes a delicious substitute for chicken. But if you are using precooked turkey remember to adjust the cooking time of the meat. Play around with this meal—it lends itself to experimenting. It also can teach you some basics of cook-ing. Our directions are for a large baking dish, but you can portion this into individual baking dishes just as easily.

  2 large onions, chopped,
  6 stalks celery, sliced
½ pound sliced mushrooms
  4 tablespoons sweet butter, melted
  1 pound carrots, peeled, sliced and parboiled
  4 Idaho potatoes. peeled, cubed and parboiled
  3 pounds chicken breasts, poached only until still pink on the
     inside, boned, skinned and cut in 1-inch cubes
1½ cups drained canned corn kernels
  1 cup frozen young peas, thawed
     White Sauce (recipe follows)
  3 cups grated Cheddar cheese
     dough for 18- by-12-inch pie crust (recipe on page 224) with
     ½ teaspoon dried basil and 1 teaspoon dried thyme and 1
     teaspoon fresh dill added
     small egg beaten with 1 tablespoon water *(continued on next page)*

Preheat oven to 325 degrees.

Sauté onions, celery and mushrooms in the butter until soft. Remove pot from heat and add carrots, potatoes, chicken, corn and peas, stirring to combine. Pour white sauce over chicken mixture, stirring until chicken is well coated. Place mixture in 18- by-12-inch baking dish and sprinkle with grated cheese.

On a lightly floured surface, roll out pie crust to 19- by-13-inch rectangle. Place over the chicken, trim and crimp the edges, and cut several vents in dough. Brush with egg wash.

Place pie on cookie sheet to catch any drips and bake 50 to 55 minutes, until golden.

WHITE SAUCE FOR CHICKEN POT PIE

MAKES
10 CUPS

Please refer to the white sauce recipe used with Macaroni and Cheese on page 61. Add 3 cups of hot chicken stock (recipe on page 48) when using white sauce with Chicken Pot Pie. Pour white sauce over chicken and vegetable mixture, stirring well.

CHICKEN BREASTS
STUFFED

with

GRUYÈRE

and

ARTICHOKE HEARTS

..

MUSHROOM
SHERRY SAUCE

..

RISOTTO

..

BAKED BEEFSTEAK
TOMATOES

.. : .. : .. : ..

S E R V E S   We feel chicken breasts served alone lack flavor,
so at Good Enough to Eat they appear in many
_____8_____ guises: cloaked in spicy sauces, cubed for hearty
stews, wrapped around piquant fillings and stuffed with sur-
prising combinations like this mixture—Gruyère and artichoke hearts—with its French overtones. Because the
breasts, when topped with the mushroom sherry sauce, tend
to be rich, we suggest serving them atop a bed of plain rice,
which soaks up the sauce. The breasts should hold up well

when stuffed, so they can be preassembled earlier in the day, then cooked just before serving time.

For the most aesthetic arrangement of this meal, slice the breasts into 3 or 4 sections, then fan them out to follow the curve of your plate by pressing on them with the palm of your hand.

The *risotto* is a simple Italian side dish for which you should use the special Italian Arborio rice, sold in Italian groceries.

STUFFED CHICKEN BREASTS

SERVES
8

14-ounce can artichoke hearts, drained, quartered
½ pound Gruyère cheese, coarsely grated
2 teaspoons chopped fresh thyme, or 1 teaspoon dried
½ teaspoon dry mustard
1 teaspoon kosher salt
½ teaspoon white pepper
1 teaspoon paprika
½ teaspoon cayenne
8 whole chicken breasts, boned, skinned, fillets removed, and pounded flat
8 teaspoons cold sweet butter
½ cup white wine

Preheat oven to 350 degrees.

Combine artichokes with cheese, thyme, mustard, salt, pepper, paprika and cayenne; set aside.

Place chicken breasts on a large baking sheet, overlapping them if necessary. Place 3 to 4 tablespoons artichoke mixture down center of each breast; top each with 1 teaspoon butter. Fold left side of breast over filling, then fold right side over left, flattening with your palms. Fold and roll breasts from the wider side, pushing in stuffing as you roll. Place breasts seam side down on baking sheet. Add wine and place any leftover stuffing on tops of breasts. Bake 20 to 25 minutes. (If you are precooking the chicken breasts, bake 15 minutes, then return to oven for 10 minutes before serving.)

MUSHROOM SHERRY SAUCE FOR STUFFED CHICKEN BREASTS

MAKES ABOUT 2½ CUPS

¼ cup sweet butter
¼ teaspoon kosher salt
13 ounces fresh mushrooms, sliced, or 8 ounces wild mushrooms (oak, or any large-capped mushroom)
¼ teaspoon ground pepper
1 tablespoon chopped fresh parsley
1 cup sherry
1 tablespoon cognac
2 cups heavy cream
1 tablespoon chopped fresh thyme

Melt 2 tablespoons butter with a pinch of salt over medium heat (for browner mushrooms omit the salt). Add mushrooms and sauté 3 minutes, then add half of parsley. Remove mushrooms to a bowl and set aside.

Add remaining 2 tablespoons butter to skillet, add the ¼ teaspoon salt and the pepper and melt over low heat.

Combine sherry with any mushroom liquid and add to pan. Turn up heat and, whisking constantly, reduce liquid by half. Add cognac and boil 1 minute. Lower heat, whisk in cream, and reduce by half. Add thyme and remaining parsley, stir in the mushrooms, and remove from heat. Sauce can be reheated carefully over low heat, if necessary, making sure it never comes to a boil.

RISOTTO

SERVES 8

4 tablespoons olive oil
1 large onion, chopped
2 medium cloves garlic, minced
3 stalks celery, chopped
1 to 2 teaspoons kosher salt
1 teaspoon ground white pepper
3 cups Italian Arborio rice
3 cups chicken stock

⅓ cup white wine
2 (or more) cups water
1 cup pitted black olives (optional)

(continued on next page)

Heat oil; add onion, garlic, celery, salt and pepper, and sweat vegetables 10 minutes, until soft but not colored. Add rice and sauté over high heat, stirring, 5 minutes. Stir in 1 cup boiling stock and the wine. Bring to a boil, reduce heat, and simmer, stirring, until liquid is absorbed. Repeat 2 more times with 1 cup stock and 1 cup water each time, until rice is creamy and all liquid is absorbed. You may need 1 additional cup of water. Add olives, if desired, when you add the last cup of liquid. If risotto is done before your main dish, cover with a damp towel.

BAKED BEEFSTEAK TOMATOES

SERVES
8

½ cup olive oil
4 small cloves garlic, minced
8 medium beefsteak tomatoes, sliced in ¼-inch-thick circles
   chopped fresh parsley for garnish

Preheat oven to 300 degrees.

Combine olive oil with garlic and brush half of mixture on baking sheet. Place tomatoes on baking sheet and brush with remaining oil and garlic. Bake 10 minutes. Garnish slices with parsley.

Seafood Meals

SHRIMP PROVENÇAL

..

HERBED RICE

..

SAUTÉED SPINACH

SERVES This robust shrimp dish is lively and vivid—a
taste experience, and just as sunny as the south-
___8___ ern French province that inspired it. It's a very
satisfying meal because it is impressive, yet simple. We've
used typical Provençal ingredients too—zucchini, garlic, tomatoes and fresh herbs. We prefer to serve the shrimps deveined but with shells on; they are more flavorful this way. If
you wish, you may use other fish such as red snapper, scallops
or lobster. You'll have leftover rice; save it and serve in a
salad the next day, or serve it reheated and mixed with meat,
vegetables, and fresh herbs. You may also have leftover garlic
butter, which can be frozen.

Careful plate arrangement creates an exciting presentation:
start with the bed of rice, spoon on the Provençal mixture,
then the shrimp, and then the spinach.

Peeling and deveining shrimp is a simple procedure. You can buy shrimp that have already been peeled and deveined, but these are more expensive. Doing it yourself is very easy once you get the hang of it. First, organize yourself: pile the uncleaned shrimp on your left side, place a large bowl for the cleaned shrimp in front of you, and place a damp paper towel for wiping off your paring knife. Then, grasp each shrimp with one hand, and with the thumb of the other unwrap the peel from the midpoint up in one circular movement. Next, pinch the tail tightly with one hand and gently extract the shrimp with the other. Place it in the bowl.

Deveining each shrimp before cooking is your next step, and one which, for aesthetics and taste, you should not omit. Uncurl the shrimp on a flat surface, and, with a small paring knife, make a very shallow head-to-tail slice along its top curve. With the knife blade, scrape out any intestines, and wipe off the knife on the damp towel.

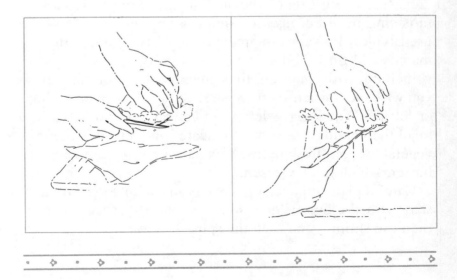

SHRIMP PROVENÇAL

 4 small cloves garlic, minced
 1 bunch fresh parsley, chopped
 1 teaspoon kosher salt
 1 teaspoon ground white pepper
1½ cups sweet butter, softened
 1 tablespoon lemon juice
 1 tablespoon white wine
40 large shrimp, about 4 pounds
   Provençal Mixture (recipe follows)

Combine the garlic, parsley, salt, pepper and butter and stir until light and fluffy. Add the lemon juice and wine. Scrape the butter onto a wax-paper-covered surface and roll it into a sausage shape. Wrap in parchment paper and refrigerate until it holds its shape.

Preheat oven to 350 degrees.

Peel and devein the shrimp. Thoroughly rinse and drain. Butterfly shrimp (see glossary for method). Place shrimp in a 12- by-9-inch ovenproof baking dish and top each with 2 to 3 teaspoons of the butter. Bake about 3 minutes, placing serving platter in oven to warm for 1 minute while shrimp are baking.

To serve, heap the Herbed Rice (recipe on page 161) in the center of a platter, surround with the Sautéed Spinach (recipe on page 161), and place the shrimp over the rice. Spoon the warm Provençal Mixture, below, over the shrimp and rice. Dot with garlic butter and serve immediately.

Zucchini is a vegetable with a large variety of uses. Likewise, it can be cut and shaped in many ways. Here are our suggestions. First, scrub each zucchini well in cold water to remove any sand. Then lay the zucchini flat on the cutting surface. With a vegetable peeler, "stripe" it lengthwise five times for a uniform shape. Then, cut off both ends. Slice the zucchini across the width, in half or in thirds. When you plan to eat zucchini raw, you will want to get rid of the seedy core, which has a bitter taste. To do this, cut off the flesh around the center to reveal the central core, and discard the core.

You can cut zucchini into different shapes for various recipes. Diagonals: rocking cuts back and forth on a slant to make thin slices; good for fish stews when you want the zucchini to be barely cooked. Julienne strips: make these from the flesh cut off the core. Cut it into matchstick-sized pieces for use in salads or cooked vegetable dishes. Circles: thin slices for cooking or eating raw. Triangular chunks: Cut the whole zucchini, core in, on opposing diagonals to form large triangles: Cubes: Cut the flesh off one side of the core and cut in two lengthwise. Stack and cut into small dice.

Incidentally, you can follow the same procedures with yellow summer squash, but with one exception. When "striping" the skin, peel it so lightly that only the very top layer, which is tough and bitter, comes off. If you have peeled it properly, the squash will retain its yellow color.

PROVENÇAL MIXTURE

MAKES
2 QUARTS

     kosher salt
4 medium zucchini
2 pounds plum tomatoes, cored and sliced in eighths
     5-ounce can pitted black olives, drained and halved
2 fourteen-ounce jars drained artichoke hearts, quartered
4 cloves garlic chopped
1 cup olive oil
1 medium onion, thinly sliced
1 tablespoon chopped fresh basil or ½ teaspoon dried
1 tablespoon chopped fresh rosemary, or ½ teaspoon dried
2 teaspoons fresh sage, or 1 teaspoon dried
1 bay leaf

½ cup white wine
1 tablespoon ground white pepper

Preheat oven to 325 degrees.

Cut zucchini into ½-inch-thick slices and degorge them. (See glossary.)

Combine all ingredients with 1 tablespoon kosher salt in a 3-quart ovenproof baking dish. Bake 1 hour, covered with foil, checking after 45 minutes to be sure vegetables do not overcook. Or cook in medium saucepan over low heat, covered, for 40 minutes.

HERBED RICE

SERVES
8
OR MORE

4 cups long-grain rice
1 teaspoon kosher salt
1 tablespoon sweet butter
1 teaspoon chopped fresh basil, or ½ teaspoon dried
1 teaspoon chopped fresh thyme, or ½ teaspoon dried
1 teaspoon chopped fresh rosemary, or ½ teaspoon dried

To prepare rice, combine all ingredients in 8 cups water and cook. (See box on page 185 for cooking method.)

SAUTÉED SPINACH

SERVES
8

2 pounds fresh spinach, approximately
4 tablespoons olive oil

2 teaspoons kosher salt
juice of 1 lemon
1 teaspoon vinegar (optional)

To clean spinach, rinse several times in tepid water with a pinch of kosher salt. Dry in a salad spinner or wrap in a towel.

Place half the oil, salt and lemon juice and vinegar, if using it, in a skillet over medium-high heat. Have platter or plates ready because the spinach cooks quickly. When the lemon juice and vinegar begin to evaporate, in about 1 minute, add half the spinach. Sauté, turning leaves to coat with oil, until only slightly wilted but not limp, about 2 minutes. Remove to plate and repeat with remaining oil, salt, lemon juice and optional vinegar and spinach.

BAKED
TILEFISH

..

CHUNKY TOMATO
SAUCE

with

MUSSELS

and

CLAMS OVER
SPAGHETTI

SERVES

4

Meaty tilefish is readily available nationwide, and inexpensive, too. If you are unfamiliar with it, tilefish tastes like a cross between lobster and scallops. It gets its name from its mottled skin, which resembles mosaic tiles. You can substitute other fish cut into steaks, such as halibut or monkfish, but whatever you select must be sturdy. If you prefer, you can grill the tilefish; we suggest using an inexpensive ridged stovetop grill and allowing 10 minutes cooking time per inch thickness of fish. In order to coordinate all the fish, remember to start cooking the shellfish about 3 minutes after the tilefish has begun to bake.

When combined on the plate, the various components of this meal are reminiscent of an Italian *zuppa di pesca*. Delicious. If you wish, serve with a radicchio-and-watercress salad with some oil and vinegar, salt and pepper, and a sprinkling of roasted walnut pieces or crumbled goat cheese.

You must clean clams, mussels and oysters before cooking them. With a stiff brush, scrub shellfish under cold running water to remove any surface mud. For mussels, remove their "beards" by pulling off the strands that stick out from the shell. Then, with a knife, scrape off any incrustations on the shell. Place in a bowl and add water to cover, ⅛ cup oats, and a pinch of salt; let stand 30 minutes. Drain and place in a bowl of fresh water and cover for 15 minutes. Drain again and prepare recipe. To shuck clams and oysters, hold the shellfish in the palm of one hand over a bowl to catch any juices, then insert the tip of a knife into the hinge, severing the muscle that holds the shell halves together. Slide the knife between the shell halves, twisting the blade to force the shells apart. Then place the clams and oysters in separate bowls, cover with cold water, and continue procedure as for mussels, as above.

TILEFISH

1 cup white wine
3 peppercorns
1 teaspoon kosher salt
2 bay leaves
   pinch of nutmeg
2 teaspoons dried basil,
   crushed
1 lemon sliced
1 carrot, peeled and
   chopped
2 stalks celery
1 onion
4 eight-ounce tilefish fillets, skin
   slashed diagonally in 3 places

SHELLFISH

1½ dozen mussels
1½ dozen cherrystone
    clams
¼ cup rolled oats
   pinch of salt
½ cup white wine
2 stalks celery, chopped
2 medium cloves garlic,
   minced

(continued on next page)

CHUNKY TOMATO SAUCE

1 large onion, chopped
4 large cloves garlic, minced
¼ cup olive oil
¼ teaspoon cayenne
1 teaspoon ground black pepper
4 stalks celery, diced
¼ cup red wine
2 to 3 red bell peppers, diced
2 pounds plum tomatoes, cored and finely diced

12 anchovies soaked 20 minutes in milk and drained
1 cup sliced halved, pitted black olives
3-ounce bottle capers, drained (optional)
1 tablespoon tomato paste
1 bay leaf
1 pound mushrooms, sliced
¼ cup chopped fresh parsley

1 pound spaghetti
2 cups freshly grated Parmesan cheese (½ pound)

Preheat oven to 400 degrees and clean shellfish according to directions on page 163.

To make Tomato Sauce, sauté onion and garlic in oil with cayenne, black pepper and celery. Sweat over low heat 15 minutes, but do not brown. Add wine and reduce it by half. Add remaining ingredients except mushrooms and parsley. Cook 15 minutes. Add mushrooms and cook 5 minutes longer. Add parsley and cook 10 minutes. Cover and keep warm.

To cook tilefish, make a *fumet* (see glossary) by combining the wine, peppercorns, salt, bay leaves, nutmeg, basil, lemon, carrot, celery and onion with 10 cups water in a large baking dish over low heat. When warm, place fish skin side down in baking dish. Place in oven and bake 10 minutes. Turn fish and bake 6 to 7 minutes longer.

Prepare spaghetti in large pot following directions for cooking pasta on page 80. Set aside in colander to cool.

To cook shellfish, place ½ cup water, the wine, celery, and garlic in empty pasta pot. Add clams and cook, covered, 3 minutes. Add mussels and cook, covered, about 6 minutes longer, until all shellfish are opened (discard any that do not open).

To reheat the spaghetti, place it in a saucepan with a little oil. Warm, covered, over very low heat.

To serve, place the reheated spaghetti in a large soup tureen. Cover with Tomato Sauce, then the tilefish. Surround with shellfish; sprinkle with Parmesan cheese to taste.

Have a bowl in the center of the table for discarded shells.

SEAFOOD STEW

with

GARLIC CROUTONS

and

ROUILLE

•••

SERVES

10

Our answer to the famous French *bouillabaisse* is this light, summery, seafood stew brimming with crunchy seasonal vegetables and sweet, tender shellfish. What's remarkable about this dish is its versatility—you can combine any seafood with any vegetable fresh from the marketplace. Constants, however, must be the Pernod and orange rind for that summery taste.

At serving time, we layer the croutons and *rouille* at the bottom of the bowl so their flavors float up to mingle with the seafood. If you wish, you can layer pasta or rice on the bottom, too. Chilled fruity white wine and a crisp green salad make this a complete meal.

SEAFOOD STEW

SERVES
10

¾ cup olive oil
3 large onions, chopped
4 bunches scallions or 3 large leeks, cleaned and thinly sliced
1 bunch celery, cleaned and sliced
4 large cloves garlic, minced
2 tablespoons kosher salt
1 tablespoon ground white pepper
½ cup Pernod

8 cups *fumet* (fish stock) or 5 cups bottled clam juice
   combined with 3 cups water
2 cups canned crushed tomatoes
2¾ pounds plum tomatoes, cored and cubed
   grated zest of 1 orange
1 tablespoon lemon juice
6 basil leaves, julienned, or 2 teaspoons dried basil
1 teaspoon dried rosemary
2 bay leaves
1 tablespoon fennel seeds
1 tablespoon chopped fresh sage or ½ teaspoon dry
4 zucchini (about ½ pound each), julienned, or sliced on the
   diagonal
10 carrots, peeled and julienned
¼ cup chopped fresh parsley
1 pound redfish, cut in 1-inch strips
1 pound bay scallops, or sea scallops halved
1 pound monkfish, cut in 1-inch strips
1 pound flounder, cut in 1-inch strips
20 large shrimp (about 2 pounds) cleaned, cut in half
30 littleneck clams, cleaned
½ cup white wine
50 mussels, cleaned

Preheat oil in a stockpot. Add onions, scallions or leeks, celery,
garlic, salt and pepper. Sweat vegetables over low heat 15 to 20
minutes. Add Pernod and reduce to ¼. Add stock or clam juice
and water, crushed tomatoes, plum tomatoes, orange zest, lemon
juice, basil, rosemary, bay leaves, fennel seeds and sage. Bring to
a boil, then lower to a simmer for 20 minutes. Stir in zucchini and
carrots and remove stockpot from heat; let stand 20 minutes, then

stir in parsley. Correct seasoning. Add fish and shrimp and simmer
5 to 10 minutes, until fish is done.

Meanwhile, place clams in large pot with 1 inch salted water and
the wine. Cook over medium heat, covered, 4 minutes, then add
mussels. Cover and cook about 7 to 8 minutes longer, until shellfish have opened (throw away any that have remained closed).
Serve on top of the stew.

---

*Leeks are delicious but very sandy; they need thorough
rinsing in cold water to remove all the grit. To prepare
them, cut off the roots at the very end. Peel off any old
green leaves and discard. Look for the big V, where the
white stem and green leafy portion meet. Use a sharp
chef's knife, and slice almost through the leek from the
root end up through the V and leaves. Open the leek up
and rinse under hard-running cold water. You must clean
every layer because of the sand trapped between them.
Otherwise, food will be sandy. Trim off any limp tips
from the green leaves, then slice all the way through the
leek along your original lengthwise cut. Rinse again in
a colander. Then, cut the leek into julienne, rounds, or
on the diagonal, as needed in the recipe.*

CROUTONS

1 cup sweet butter
1 large clove garlic, chopped
1 tablespoon chopped fresh
  parsley
  pinch each salt and pepper
1 teaspoon lemon juice

1 loaf day-old French bread,
  sliced diagonally in ½-inch-
  thick slices
  grated Parmesan cheese
  (optional) for sprinkling

Preheat oven to 450 degrees.

Combine butter with garlic, parsley, salt, pepper, and lemon
juice in saucepan over low heat. Place bread slices on a baking

sheet and brush on both sides with butter mixture. Sprinkle each slice with cheese, if desired. Bake 10 to 15 minutes, until golden.

ROUILLE

MAKES
ABOUT
5 CUPS

  3 egg yolks
  2 teaspoons salt
  1 to 2 teaspoons ground white pepper
¼ teaspoon paprika
  1 tablespoon Dijon mustard
  4 cloves garlic, minced
  4 red bell peppers, roasted, peeled, chopped, and well dried
  4 teaspoons cayenne fried in 1 tablespoon butter for 3 minutes
     (this will eliminate any bitterness in the cayenne)
¼ cup freshly squeezed lemon juice
½ teaspoon hot pepper sauce
  4 cups olive oil

Place bowl on damp towel so it will not move, if you are making by hand. Place yolks in bowl, or in blender or food processor; add salt, pepper, paprika, mustard, garlic, bell peppers and cayenne. Whisk well, scraping down sides of bowl, until well blended. Whisking continuously, drizzle in lemon juice and hot pepper sauce, then very slowly drizzle in the oil. Mixture should start to thicken when half the oil has been added. Whisk until all the oil is incorporated.

SPICY CATFISH

with

TOMATO-ONION-
KETCHUP SAUCE

..

CREAMED SPINACH

..

NEW POTATOES

with

BACON AND ONIONS

SERVES Catfish, ugly and often neglected in fancy kitchens, yield surprisingly sweet, tender flesh. Since
_____8_____ catfish contain many tiny bones and are hard to
clean, buy fillets from your fish dealer. In some parts of the
country, catfish is hard to find, so you can substitute gray
sole, or other sweet fish. You need the sweetness to stand up
to the spicy batter, an idea we picked up from Cajun recipes.
To time this dinner correctly, begin sautéing the catfish right
after you add the drained spinach to the cream mixture.

SPICY CATFISH

1 cup all-purpose flour
2 tablespoons kosher salt
3 tablespoons black pepper
2 teaspoons cayenne
1 teaspoon paprika
1 tablespoon chili powder

2 teaspoons dry mustard
8 eight-ounce fillets of catfish
8 tablespoons sweet butter
4 tablespoons olive oil

In a large bowl, combine the flour, salt, pepper, cayenne, paprika, chili powder and mustard, blending well.

Make 3 diagonal slashes on the skin side of each fillet about 1 inch long and ⅛ inch deep. Dredge fillets in flour mixture and shake off excess. Place fillets on a baking sheet. (This should be done just prior to cooking, otherwise flour will become pasty.)

In a 10-inch skillet, heat the butter and oil until bubbling, shaking the skillet. Add fillets, skin side down, the thickest part of the fish touching the fat first. Continue shaking the skillet. (Cook the fish in 2 batches to avoid overcrowding.) Cook fish on first side for about 4 minutes, depending on thickness, then turn to cook other side for 4 minutes, until done. Have plates warming in the oven on warm.

While the fish is cooking, reheat the Tomato-Onion-Ketchup Sauce (recipe follows) over low heat. During the last 3 minutes of cooking time, place the New Potatoes with Bacon and Onions (page 172) in the oven to reheat. To serve, place a spoonful of sauce on each fillet, then surround the fish with Creamed Spinach (page 172) on one side, potatoes on the other.

◇ · ◇ · ◇ · ◇ · ◇ · ◇ · ◇ · ◇ · ◇ ·

Seafood is super-delicate, and if you sauté it the cooking time will be quick. Always protect any seafood with seasoned flours—but not thick batters, which will only slow cooking time. If you want a dark-brown crust, sprinkle salt and pepper into the pan first. Cook fish on the skin side first: this is prettier, and helps hold the fish together. Remember to slash the skin in 3 places first—

slashes should be 1 inch long, 1/8 inch deep—otherwise the fish will burst or buckle as the cooking skin tightens. We undercook fish very slightly so it is not dry and tasteless. As a rule of thumb, cooking time is 10 minutes per inch at the thickest part of the piece of fish.

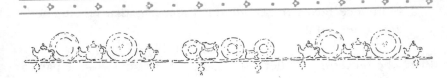

TOMATO-ONION-KETCHUP SAUCE

MAKES
ABOUT
2 CUPS

 4 tablespoons sweet butter
 2 teaspoons kosher salt
 1 teaspoon ground black pepper
 ½ teaspoon cayenne
 2 large onions, halved and thinly sliced
 2 large cloves garlic, minced
 1 tablespoon red wine
 2 teaspoons freshly squeezed lemon juice
 1 tablespoon tomato paste
 1 tablespoon hot pepper sauce
 1 tablespoon Dijon mustard
 2 cups ketchup
 2 teaspoons Worcestershire sauce
 1 bunch fresh parsley, chopped

Melt the butter over medium heat. Add salt, pepper and cayenne and sauté 2 minutes. Add the onions and garlic, stirring occasionally. Allow the onions to stick and get slightly brown. Drizzle in the wine and lemon juice and deglaze brown spots on the bottom of the skillet until liquid has evaporated. When the onions are soft and brown, stir in tomato paste, hot pepper sauce, mustard, ketchup, Worcestershire sauce and parsley. Lower the heat and simmer 15 minutes, stirring often. Transfer sauce to saucepan and set aside.

CREAMED SPINACH

SERVES
8

1 cup sweet butter, cut up
2 teaspoons kosher salt
2 teaspoons ground black pepper
1 teaspoon paprika
2 cups heavy cream
2 ten-ounce boxes frozen chopped spinach, thawed, drained, and squeezed dry

Place the butter in a skillet over medium heat and swirl the pan to let the butter bronze. (This will impart the aroma of roasted nuts.) Add the salt, pepper and paprika. Add the cream, stirring constantly, and let cook for about 8 minutes, until cream is reduced by half and coats the back of a spoon. Stir in the spinach and cook 1 to 2 minutes longer. Remove from heat.

When ready to serve, reheat the spinach for 10 minutes; do not overcook or the spinach will discolor.

NEW POTATOES WITH BACON AND ONIONS

SERVES
8

1½ pounds bacon, cut in ½-inch pieces
2 medium Spanish onions (about ¾ pound), thinly sliced
1 tablespoon sweet butter
½ teaspoon salt
2 teaspoons ground black pepper
4 pounds new potatoes, parboiled and sliced in ⅛-inch circles
2 to 3 tablespoons chopped fresh parsley

Sauté bacon over medium heat for 5 minutes, until crisp. Drain off all but 1 tablespoon of the fat. Add onions and black pepper and sauté, stirring, 10 minutes, until onions are brown. Stir in the butter and salt.

Add the potatoes but do not crowd the skillet (make in 2 batches if necessary). Sauté about 10 minutes, or until the potatoes are golden brown and crunchy. Stir in the parsley. Set potatoes aside. Correct seasonings.

BAKED RED SNAPPER

with

BLACK BEAN SAUCE

..

STIR-FRIED VEGETABLES

..

SAFFRON RICE

S E R V E S Despite its obvious Chinese influences, this entire meal is really eclectic. We use canned black
_____8_____ American beans, and saffron—Spanish? Portu-
guese? Pennsylvania Dutch?—to spark the white rice. Although we call for Chinese vegetables—snow peas, scallions
and green peppers—you can substitute any other vegetables
for stir-frying, such as broccoli, zucchini or sugar snap peas.
Remember to prepare all your vegetables for stir-frying before beginning to prepare any other parts of this dinner. The
whole meal with its vibrant colors is dramatic, for both the
eyes and the taste buds.

BAKED RED SNAPPER
WITH BLACK BEAN SAUCE

SERVES
6

BLACK BEAN SAUCE

MAKES
3 CUPS

    2 tablespoons sweet butter
    2 large cloves garlic, chopped
       ½-inch piece fresh ginger, peeled and chopped
    2 large red bell peppers, diced
    1 teaspoon kosher salt
    1 teaspoon ground black pepper
    2 tablespoons lemon juice
 1½ cups white wine
  ½ cup chopped fresh parsley
       16-ounce can black beans

To make Black Bean Sauce, melt butter in saucepan; add garlic, ginger, bell peppers, salt and pepper, and sauté 5 minutes. Add the lemon juice, wine, and parsley, and reduce liquid to one quarter of its original volume. Stir in beans and cook over low heat for 10 minutes, stirring occasionally.

BAKED RED SNAPPER

    1 cup white wine
    2 teaspoons kosher salt
    6 white peppercorns
    5 sprigs fresh thyme, or 2 teaspoons dried
    2 tablespoons chopped fresh parsley
    2 tablespoons paprika
    2 lemons, thinly sliced
    8 eight-ounce red snapper fillets or small whole red snappers

    1 lemon cut in 6 wedges
    2 tablespoons chopped parsley
    2 tablespoons paprika

Preheat oven to 425 degrees.

To make fish, combine wine, salt, peppercorns, thyme, parsley, paprika and lemon slices in an 18-by-12-inch baking pan. Place over medium heat until warmed, then add fish, skin side down. Place in oven and bake about 15 minutes, or until flesh flakes easily when tested with a fork. Remove fish to plate.

Dip one side of each lemon wedge into chopped parsley, and the other into paprika. Spoon Black Bean Sauce over fish and garnish with the lemon wedges.

STIR-FRIED VEGETABLES WITH SOY SAUCE AND SESAME SEEDS

SERVES
8

½ pound snow peas, cleaned, strings removed
½ pound mushrooms, cleaned and sliced
1 bunch broccoli cut into florets, stems cut in thin slices
4 scallions, thinly sliced
⅓ cup vegetable oil
1 tablespoon soy sauce
1 tablespoon sesame seeds

Combine vegetables in a large bowl.

Heat oil, soy sauce and sesame seeds in wok. When oil is bubbling, add vegetables and stir-fry 3 to 4 minutes.

SAFFRON RICE

SERVES
8

2 teaspoons saffron threads
3 cups long-grain rice
1 tablespoon olive oil
pinch of kosher salt

In a saucepan, bring 6 cups water to a boil; remove ½ cup and combine with saffron threads to soften. Return saffron-water to saucepan, add rice, olive oil, and salt, and cook, covered, according to directions for cooking rice on page 185.

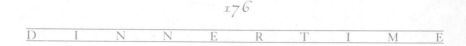
MARINATED
DILL SALMON

with

MUSTARD SAUCE

..

JULIENNED
VEGETABLES

..

WILD RICE

SERVES Most people adore salmon, despite its exorbitant
8   cost. Whenever possible, purchase fresh rather
than frozen salmon. And use steaks rather than
fillets, because they stand up better to lengthy marinating.
Allow the steaks to marinate several hours so they can absorb
the pungent oil-herb mixture.

Nutty-tasting wild rice is costly, but a delicious addition to
this meal. Many people think it is too hard to prepare, but
once you have added all the flavoring ingredients to the
water, you cook wild rice—which is not a rice at all, but a
wild grass—just like white rice. For extra flavor, we add a
ham hock to the cooking water. You can use olive oil instead,
but it doesn't taste quite as wonderful.

MARINATED DILL SALMON, BAKED OR GRILLED

SERVES
8

dill

    large bunch fresh dill
1¼ cups olive oil
 ¼ to ½ cup coarse-grain mustard
 ½ cup soy sauce
 ½ cup honey
 1 tablespoon Worcestershire sauce
 1 tablespoon brown sugar
 2 teaspoons ground black pepper
 2 medium cloves garlic, crushed
 1 large onion, sliced
 2 lemons, sliced into circles, stuck with 3 whole cloves in the centers
 1 cup white wine or sherry
 1 teaspoon ground ginger (optional)
 1 teaspoon anise seeds (optional)

 8 eight-ounce salmon steaks
 3 tablespoons chopped fresh parsley for garnish

Chop half the bunch of dill; reserve other half for garnish.

Combine 1 cup oil with chopped dill and remaining ingredients, except lemon slices, parsley and salmon. Mix until well combined. Add salmon and marinate, refrigerated, for 3 hours, turning occasionally. Preheat oven to 400 degrees.

Brush 2 large baking dishes with remaining oil. Arrange salmon in dishes; add a half inch of marinade. Bake, broil, or grill salmon about 4 minutes each side. Dip 1 side of each lemon slice in parsley; place 2 to 3 slices lemon, parsley side up, overlapping on fish. Garnish with sprig of dill on the side.

JULIENNED VEGETABLES

SERVES
8

2 carrots, peeled and julienned
3 celery stalks, halved crosswise and julienned
4 tablespoons butter
1 teaspoon kosher salt
1 teaspoon pepper
2 small zucchini, seeded and julienned
2 cucumbers, peeled, quartered and seeded
8 to 10 cherry tomatoes

2 tablespoons chopped fresh parsley for garnish

Blanch carrots and celery. Melt butter over medium heat; add salt and pepper. Add remaining vegetables and cook over medium heat, stirring, 2 minutes. Garnish with parsley and serve immediately.

◇ ▪ ◇ ▪ ◇ ▪ ◇ ▪ ◇ ▪ ◇ ▪ ◇ ▪ ◇ ▪ ◇ ▪

Sautéing is a wonderful way to prepare julienned vegetables. First, blanch the vegetables in some boiling water, or they will still be raw after sautéing. Then melt just enough butter to coat the bottom of your sauté pan or skillet and the vegetables. Try not to use more than 2 tablespoons of butter for 4 portions of vegetables or the vegetables will be oily. It's easiest to use tongs to sauté and remove the food from the pan. In fact, we use them so much they have become like extensions of our arms. Tongs are also best because you can easily pick the vegetables up, let the extra butter drip off them, and place them expertly on the plates. Two tips: don't add salt to your sauté until the last few moments, or it may cause the butter to burn; and remember not to overcook the vegetables or they will be limp and unattractive.

◇ ▪ ◇ ▪ ◇ ▪ ◇ ▪ ◇ ▪ ◇ ▪ ◇ ▪ ◇ ▪ ◇ ▪

WILD RICE

SERVES

8

- 1 medium ham hock
- 1 large onion stuck with 3 whole cloves
- 2 cloves garlic
- 2 teaspoons black pepper, ground
- 1 tablespoon kosher salt
- 3 cups wild rice, washed and drained
- 2 tablespoons olive oil

Bring 9 cups water to a boil with ham hock—or, if unavailable, 2 tablespoons olive oil—onion, garlic, pepper and 2 teaspoons of the salt. Stir in rice with wooden spoon. Reduce heat as low as possible, cover pot, and simmer rice 30 to 40 minutes, until tender. Remove ham hock and onion and rinse under hot water, then mix with remaining teaspoon salt and the olive oil.

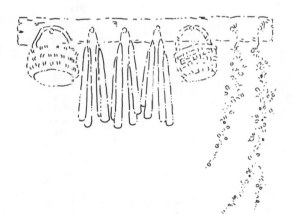

BAKED TUNA NIÇOISE

with

BOILED POTATOES

..

OLIVES

..

ANCHOVIES

..

TOMATOES

and

SPINACH

SERVES This fabulous dish was inspired by our luncheon
pain bagna, a spicy Niçoise combination of
8 garlic, tomatoes, olives, and anchovies—all the
delectable flavors of Nice.

Fresh tuna has a beautiful deep red color, lovely with the
sauce. Fresh, not canned, tuna is a must for this recipe, and
if you cannot find it, substitute swordfish for the tuna.

TUNA OR SWORDFISH STEAKS

S E R V E S
8

8 eight-ounce tuna or swordfish steaks
Almost Pesto (page 182) or olive oil
2 lemons, cut in wedges

To bake or broil fish, preheat oven to 425 degrees, or preheat broiler. Line baking sheet with aluminum foil; butter the foil.

Brush fish on both sides with Almost Pesto; place on prepared baking sheet. Bake or broil 4 to 5 minutes. Turn, brush again with Almost Pesto, and cook for 5 minutes longer.

To grill fish, heat grill to very high. Brush fish with olive oil. Grill 2 minutes on each side. Turn again to make grill marks on each side.

NIÇOISE SAUTÉ

S E R V E S
8

2 pounds new potatoes, parboiled, cooled and quartered
10½-ounce can chickpeas, drained
2 green bell peppers, julienned
2 red bell peppers, julienned
½ pound Niçoise olives
5 canned artichoke hearts, halved (14-ounce can)
2 pounds plum tomatoes, cut in eighths
1 pound mushrooms, sliced
2 teaspoons chopped fresh thyme, or 1 teaspoon dried
2 teaspoons chopped fresh sage, or 1 teaspoon dried
1 teaspoon chopped fresh marjoram, or ½ teaspoon dried
2 teaspoons kosher salt
2 teaspoons ground black pepper
3 to 4 tablespoons oil from top of Almost Pesto (recipe below)
4 hard-cooked eggs, cut in wedges (optional)

2 tablespoons olive oil
2 pounds fresh spinach, cleaned and dried
½ pound Parmesan cheese, freshly grated (2 cups)
8 eight-ounce tuna or swordfish steaks, cooked
2 lemons, cut in wedges   *(continued on next page)*

Combine all Niçoise Sauté ingredients except oil, eggs, spinach and Parmesan cheese in a large bowl. Ten to 15 minutes before serving, heat this oil in large skillet. Add all ingredients except eggs; sauté just until heated through, 5 to 7 minutes. Remove from heat and add eggs, if using, then plate.

Heat olive oil in skillet. Add spinach and stir until just wilted. Plate spinach and top with Parmesan cheese.

Serve with tuna or swordfish steaks. Drizzle everything with Almost Pesto (make sure it is well stirred first). Garnish with lemon wedges.

ALMOST PESTO

YIELDS
ABOUT
2 CUPS

1 large bunch fresh basil, chopped
4 medium cloves garlic, minced
1 cup chopped walnut pieces
1 teaspoon kosher salt
1 teaspoon ground white pepper
½ teaspoon dry mustard
½ teaspoon paprika
2 two-ounce cans anchovies, drained, soaked in milk, drained, and chopped
2 tablespoons lemon juice
1½ cups olive oil
3-ounce jar capers, drained (optional)

basil

On a cutting board, combine basil, garlic and walnut pieces. Add salt, pepper, mustard, paprika and anchovies. Chop all ingredients until blended. Transfer to medium bowl.

Sprinkle with lemon juice, then drizzle on the oil and stir well to combine. Stir in capers, if desired.

Let the pesto macerate, covered, in the refrigerator for at least 1½ hours before serving. Don't worry if it separates. Simply stir to recombine.

STUFFED BEER-BATTER SHRIMP

..

LEMON RICE

..

BLUE CHEESE MAYONNAISE

SERVES Shrimp and crabmeat are both subtly sweet and
make a delectable vehicle for our full-flavored
8 beer batter. When fried and dunked into the
blue cheese mayo, the battered shrimp stuffed with crabmeat
are exceptional. This recipe is also an obvious example of our
crusty-mushy food theory—the batter provides the crust and
the shrimp are both soft and chewy. If you are avoiding fried
foods, you can bake this entree instead, but omit the batter.
This would also be excellent served as an appetizer.

STUFFED BEER-BATTER SHRIMP

½ cup sweet butter
1 teaspoon kosher salt
¼ teaspoon ground white pepper
¼ teaspoon paprika
   pinch of cayenne
¼ teaspoon dry mustard
¼ cup bread crumbs
½ cup all-purpose flour
1 cup white wine
2 tablespoons lemon juice
2 cloves garlic, minced
1 cup milk, warmed to scalding
¼ teaspoon dried thyme
2 tablespoons chopped fresh parsley
1 tablespoon chopped fresh dill
½ pound crab meat
⅓ cup grated Parmesan cheese
32 large shrimp (about 3 pounds)
   Beer Batter (recipe follows)
   pinch of kosher salt for sprinkling finished shrimp

dill

thyme

Heat butter with salt, pepper, paprika, cayenne and mustard and cook 5 minutes over low heat. Add bread crumbs and cook over medium-low heat 3 minutes longer. Stir in flour and cook, stirring, 2 minutes longer. Add wine, lemon juice and garlic and reduce liquid almost completely, stirring often. Slowly add milk, thyme, parsley, and dill. Cook, stirring, about 5 minutes, until thick. Add crab meat; cook about 10 minutes longer. Stir in cheese. Cool for 20 minutes and refrigerate while cleaning shrimp. Line large bowl with paper towels.

Clean shrimp. Butterfly shrimp, making sure not to pierce shrimp all the way through. Place shrimp on baking sheet. Place about 2 tablespoons crab-meat filling on each shrimp, patting down to secure filling. Refrigerate until firm, about 45 minutes.

Heat oil to 375 degrees in medium saucepan. Holding each shrimp by the tail, dip it into the batter. Fry 2 to 3 minutes each side, until golden. Transfer to paper-towel-lined bowl and sprinkle with a little kosher salt for a crisper coating.

BEER BATTER

  1 cup all-purpose flour
  1 teaspoon baking powder
  1 teaspoon salt
  1 teaspoon ground white pepper
1¼ cups flat beer
  1 tablespoon vegetable oil

Combine flour, baking powder, salt and pepper. Make a well in the mixture and pour in beer and oil. Combine gradually. Do not overmix. Let rest 15 to 30 minutes before using.

This is also good to use for vegetables, fish or chicken.

Cooking rice falls into its own special category, because rice does not poach, boil or simmer, but cooks at a temperature even lower than a simmer. For white rice, use the following ratio: 1 cup of uncooked rice to 2 cups of water. Put the water into a saucepan with a pinch of salt and 2 tablespoons butter, then stir in the rice, and bring it to a boil. Once boiling, reduce the heat to very low and cover the pan. Do not stir. Just check once or twice to see if there's still enough water. Once almost all the water has cooked away, after around 15 to 18 minutes, turn off the heat, leave the cover on the pot and let it sit for a few minutes. Fluff rice up with a fork before serving.

For brown rice, follow package directions for water quantities and cook just like white rice. If you want, you can fry white or brown rice first before cooking it in water.

LEMON RICE

¼ cup white wine
  juice and grated zest of 3 lemons
1 tablespoon sweet butter
  pinch of salt
4 cups water
2 cups long-grain rice

Bring wine, lemon juice and zest, butter, salt and water to a boil. Pour in rice. For cooking rice, follow instructions on page 185.

BLUE CHEESE MAYONNAISE

MAKES
3 TO 4
CUPS

4 ounces blue cheese or gorgonzola
½ cup olive oil
2 teaspoons minced garlic
1 teaspoon kosher salt
1 teaspoon ground black pepper
2 drops hot pepper sauce
¼ teaspoon paprika
1 teaspoon Dijon mustard
2 teaspoons tomato paste
2 teaspoons lemon juice
½ cup ketchup
1 cup Mayonnaise (recipe on page 63)
2 tablespoons sour cream
2 tablespoons chopped fresh parsley

Combine ¼ cup olive oil, the garlic, salt, pepper, hot sauce, paprika, mustard, tomato paste, in a saucepan. Cook over very low heat 10 to 15 minutes. Pour mixture into a bowl to cool.

When mixture has cooled, whisk in lemon juice, mustard, ketchup, mayonnaise, sour cream, and remaining oil. If mixture is runny, add mayonnaise or oil to thicken. Stir in the parsley.

NOTE:
Leftovers can be used as a spread for toast or sandwiches.

CODFISH CAKES

with

TOMATO
MAYONNAISE

..

OUR
BAKED BEANS

..

CORN SLAW

S E R V E S   A traditional Friday night dinner around Boston,
codfish cakes are easy to prepare. You can use
___4___   fresh or leftover cod, mash all ingredients together, and pan fry. If you wish, make a hefty lunch sandwich
with these cod cakes.

Quite simply, our baked beans are a truly delectable and
easy dish. However, keep in mind that these baked beans
need to be soaked overnight, and need 6 to 8 hours of baking
time, so start planning this meal a day in advance. And no
New England dinner would be complete without a fresh vegetable slaw served alongside.

CODFISH CAKES

SERVES
4

1 to 1¼ pounds codfish fillets
2 cups mashed potatoes
2 large eggs
2 stalks celery, minced
    medium-sized red onion, minced
½ cup bread crumbs
¼ cup chopped fresh parsley
1 teaspoon salt
1 teaspoon white pepper
¼ teaspoon ground ginger
¼ teaspoon cayenne
½ teaspoon dry mustard
2 teaspoons lemon juice
½ cup clarified sweet butter

In large skillet poach fish in water to cover until fish flakes easily, about 8 minutes. Remove fish from water and pat dry; separate into flakes.

In a large mixing bowl, combine codfish with remaining ingredients except butter, stirring just until blended. Shape into round cakes. Refrigerate 1 hour so fish cakes will hold their shape better when frying.

Heat butter in skillet and sauté fish cakes 4 to 6 minutes, until golden on one side. Turn and sauté 4 to 6 minutes, until second side is golden.

TOMATO MAYONNAISE

MAKES
3 TO 4
CUPS

½ cup olive oil
2 teaspoons minced garlic
1 teaspoon kosher salt
1 teaspoon ground black pepper
2 drops hot pepper sauce
¼ teaspoon paprika
2 teaspoons tomato paste
2 medium tomatoes, chopped
2 teaspoons lemon juice

2 teaspoons Dijon mustard or coarse black-pepper mustard
¼ cup ketchup
1 cup Mayonnaise (recipe on page 63)
2 tablespoons sour cream
2 tablespoons chopped fresh parsley

Combine ¼ cup olive oil, the garlic, salt, pepper, hot sauce, paprika, tomatoes and tomato paste in a saucepan. Cook over very low heat 10 to 15 minutes, or until tomatoes are soft but still hold their shape. Pour mixture into a bowl to cool.

When mixture has cooled, whisk in lemon juice, mustard, ketchup, mayonnaise, sour cream, and remaining oil. If mixture is runny, add mayonnaise or oil to thicken. Stir in the parsley.

NOTE:
Leftovers can be used as a spread for toast or sandwiches.)

Our Baked Beans

SERVES
8 TO 10

1½ pounds dried navy beans
2 large onions, sliced
6 tablespoons sweet butter
½ cup maple syrup
2 tablespoons salt
1 tablespoon ground pepper
2 tablespoons Dijon mustard
½ cup ketchup
1 tablespoon tomato paste
2 tablespoons brown sugar

Wash beans several times and soak overnight in water to cover. When ready to bake them, drain and discard soaking water. Preheat oven to 300 degrees.

Place beans in saucepan; add fresh water to cover. Cook over medium heat about 45 minutes, just until skins begin to wrinkle and fall away from beans. Drain; reserve cooking liquid, adding water to equal 4 cups, if necessary.

In skillet, sauté onions in butter until slightly browned and translucent. Combine remaining ingredients. Spoon all ingredients into a 4-quart bean pot or ovenproof dish; cover with lid or aluminum foil. Bake about 6 to 8 hours, adding liquid if necessary to keep beans moist.

CORN SLAW

    small head green cabbage, about 1 pound, shredded
1 green bell pepper, chopped
1 red bell pepper, chopped
3 scallions, thinly sliced
2 carrots, peeled and julienned
2 stalks celery, thinly and diagonally sliced
    16-ounce can corn kernels, drained
½ cup sour cream
½ cup Mayonnaise (recipe on page 63)
⅛ cup red wine
1 teaspoon salt
½ teaspoon ground white pepper
    pinch of dry mustard
1 tablespoon lemon juice
¼ teaspoon paprika

In large bowl combine cabbage, bell peppers, scallions, carrots, celery and corn.

In small bowl, whisk sour cream with mayonnaise, wine, salt, pepper, mustard, lemon juice and paprika. Stir into cabbage mixture until vegetables are well coated.

4

HOLIDAY MEALS

Only a handful of commemorative holidays mark our national calendar, and Americans celebrate them with zeal and abandon. Often these national holidays are the only times during the year when close friends and family members unite, becoming living characters in Norman Rockwell's art and re-creating the American dream of cozy home and hearth. For all of us, these holidays, whether lively or solemn, mean indulgence and lavish cooking—a chance to say "I love you" with roast turkey, glazed ham or filet mignon, and, of course, all the holiday trimmings. Besides doing their culinary stint, cooks busy themselves airing out the linens and dusting off the family sterling, crystal and china—or at least, the family best—to set a splendid table. Extra touches, like fresh flowers and candles, enhance the meal.

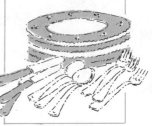

At Good Enough to Eat, we celebrate, too, with traditional recipes slightly altered to take on their own luster. Most of our holiday meals will feed more than the basic family unit and a sprinkling of friends. Besides, few home cooks should spend hours preparing festive foods without making enough for delectable leftovers.

Our bill of holiday fare celebrates such major days as Thanksgiving, Christmas and New Year's Eve; we also give tribute to several minor holidays such as St. Patrick's Day and Father's Day.

Thanksgiving

Considered by many as the ultimate bountiful meal, this patriotic feast commemorates all that Americans should feel grateful for, including our fertile lands that produce a cornucopia of crops and livestock. There really is no more perfect holiday during the year for copious cooking and overeating. How appropriate that it starts off the winter season with its string of perpetual parties.

ROAST TURKEY

with

BREAD STUFFING
AND GRAVY

MASHED RUTABAGAS

CREAMED
DILLED PEAS

CRANBERRY RELISH

SERVES
6 TO 8

Turkey and Thanksgiving are synonymous. Even if you hate turkey, can't cook it properly, or eat it twice a month all year, turkey should still be the traditional underpinning of this dinner. It is a simple bird to roast, and if you follow our tips, it will never come to the table dried out and tasteless. We recommend that you start with fresh turkey, now readily available nationwide, because you can never know how long a frozen turkey has been at market.

Turkey stuffings are popular too, and our recipe came from Ann's mother. We added nuts for crunchiness, apple cider for a hint of sweetness, and raisins, prunes or apricots for their special taste.

Many cooks are daunted by the size and seeming difficulty of preparing the rutabaga, yet this flavorful turnip should turn up, if possible, at Thanksgiving dinner. Our mashed rutabagas, seasoned with cinnamon and salt pork, combine northern and southern cookery for a traditional-style holiday vegetable dish.

Creamed dill peas, redolent of cream, butter and chopped dill, plus an orangey cranberry relish, round out the meal.

ROAST TURKEY

SERVES
6 TO 8
(OR MORE)

14- to 16-pound turkey with giblets,
    fresh if possible
1 cup sweet butter, cut into cubes
    kosher salt
    ground black pepper

Preheat oven to 400 degrees.

Remove giblets and neck from turkey cavity and place them in an 18-by-24-inch roasting pan.

Remove excess fat from inside turkey, and rub the turkey outside and inside with salt and pepper. Place turkey in roasting pan.

Press butter cubes onto various places on the turkey. Place turkey in oven and cook 20 minutes. Baste the turkey and lower temperature to 300 degrees. Roast turkey from 2 hours and 40 minutes to 3 hours, depending on weight, basting every 15 minutes. Test for doneness by pricking the leg; if the juices run clear, the turkey is done. Place turkey on carving board and let sit for 15 to 20 minutes. Remember to reserve the giblets, neck, liver, and drippings for the gravy (recipe follows).

TURKEY GRAVY

    giblets, liver, and neck from turkey
½ cup drippings, reserved from turkey
4 tablespoons all-purpose flour
1 teaspoon kosher salt
½ teaspoon white pepper
¼ teaspoon paprika
4 cups turkey or chicken stock
3 tablespoons chopped fresh parsley

Place turkey on carving board to rest. Place giblets, liver and neck on cutting board. Trim rough parts of giblets, cut up liver and shred meat from neck. Place all this back in roaster with drippings, over medium heat. Whisk in flour and spices. Cook 4 minutes, being careful not to burn flour. Whisk in stock. Bring to a boil, reduce heat and simmer, whisking regularly, for 10 minutes.

BREAD STUFFING

2 one-pound loaves day-old white bread,
    or 2 pounds day-old French bread
2 cups apple cider
2 large onions, chopped
6 stalks celery, chopped
6 apples, peeled, cored and cut in chunks
6 tablespoons sweet butter
1½ cups chicken stock
¾ cup raisins or chopped prunes
2 teaspoons kosher salt
1 teaspoon white pepper
½ teaspoon thyme
½ teaspoon paprika
¼ teaspoon allspice
1 teaspoon sage
3 eggs, lightly beaten
½ cup walnut or pecan pieces
½ cup dried apricots, chopped
¾ cup dried plums or raisins, or 1½ cups cooked crumbled
    sausage

Preheat oven to 300 degrees.

Remove crusts from bread; cut bread into 1-inch cubes or slices and place on cookie sheet. Toast in oven until bread is light brown. Remove and place in large bowl.

Add apple cider and let it soak into bread. Add remaining ingredients and mix well. Stuff your turkey, place excess stuffing into greased ovenproof baking dish. If using baking dish, cover with foil and bake 45 minutes. Remove foil and bake uncovered the last 15 minutes for a crustier top.

MASHED RUTABAGAS

S E R V E S
6 TO 8

   2 rutabagas, about 4 pounds total, peeled and cubed
  ½ pound salt pork, cut into ¼-inch pieces
   4 tablespoons sweet butter
   1 teaspoon white pepper
  ½ teaspoon salt
  ½ teaspoon cinnamon

Place the cubed rutabagas in a saucepan and cover with water. Bring water to boil and cook rutabagas over medium heat, uncovered, for 30 to 35 minutes, or until fork-tender.

Meanwhile, place the cut-up salt pork into a skillet and fry over medium heat until brown and crisp. When rutabagas are tender, drain and return them to saucepan. Then mash them well and combine with the salt pork, drippings, butter, salt, pepper and cinnamon, stirring well. Serve immediately; or prepare ahead and reheat in a covered ovenproof dish for 15 minutes at 300 degrees.

CREAMED DILLED PEAS

dill

 2   to 3 tablespoons sweet butter
1½   teaspoons kosher salt
 1   teaspoon ground white pepper
2¼   pounds frozen petit pois, thawed
 3   tablespoons chopped fresh dill
     grated zest of 1 lemon
 1   teaspoon lemon juice

Melt butter over low heat with salt and pepper. Add the peas, dill, lemon zest and juice. Sauté 10 to 15 minutes, or until peas are warmed through. Serve with slotted spoon.

CRANBERRY RELISH

 2   twelve-ounce bags cranberries
 1   cup granulated sugar
¾   cup firmly packed brown sugar
¼   cup raspberry or strawberry preserves
 2   oranges, zest grated, pith removed, and cut in wedges
¾   teaspoon cinnamon
½   teaspoon ground cloves
¼   cup orange or apple juice
 1   tablespoon lemon juice

Place everything in saucepan; bring to a simmer. Stir, reduce heat to low, and cook 15 to 20 minutes, until cranberries are only slightly crushed or popped. Preferably, let relish sit at room temperature for at least 2 hours before serving. Serve at room temperature.

Christmas

❋❋❋❋❋❋❋❋❋❋❋❋❋❋❋❋❋❋❋❋❋❋❋❋

ROAST GOOSE

with

WILD RICE

and

FRUIT STUFFING

✳

BRAISED
RED CABBAGE

✳

CREAMED
PEARL ONIONS

❋❋❋❋❋❋❋❋❋❋❋❋❋❋❋❋❋❋❋❋❋❋❋❋

SERVES Our Christmas dinner is a heavy, richly colored meal calling for seasonal ingredients and suitable for a blustery winter day.

6

A roast goose makes a sumptuous main course for this joyous day. Although geese are very fatty and can be tricky to handle, we have overcome this by degreasing the roasting pan often. We also use a tart fruit and nut stuffing that helps cut the fatty taste. If you can find one, buy a fresh goose, rather than a frozen.

In Scandinavian countries, braised red cabbage is a traditional accompaniment to Christmas goose. To this colorful dish, we add sliced green Granny Smith apples and a sprinkling of caraway seeds for an extra festive touch. The creamed pearl onions, which lose their pungency after cooking, provide a smooth, creamy counterpoint to the dark crisp goose, and tart-sweet cabbage.

CHRISTMAS GOOSE

    10- to-11-pound goose, skin pricked with knife
2 cups water
2 cups fresh orange juice
1 cup strawberry or raspberry jam or orange marmalade
2 teaspoons fresh lemon juice

Preheat oven to 425 degrees.

Meanwhile, fill stockpot half full of water and bring to a boil. Place colander over stockpot, place goose in colander and, with foil, make a tent over the goose. Steam 20 minutes. This is to render some of the goose fat. An alternate method is to submerge goose in boiling water for 10 minutes, then drain.

Place a baking sheet face down in a 12- by-18-inch roaster. Pour in 2 cups water and the orange juice. Set the goose on the baking sheet. Make a glaze by combining the jam with the lemon juice. Brush the goose with this mixture. Roast 20 minutes, then turn temperature down to 300 degrees and cook 3 hours and 10 minutes longer, brushing with glaze every 30 minutes and basting every hour. Let stand for 10 to 15 minutes before carving.

STUFFING FOR GOOSE

    3 cups washed wild rice
    1 spiced-orange tea bag
  ½ cup dark raisins
  ½ cup golden raisins
    1 cup pitted prunes
    1 cup dried apricots
    1 cup dry sherry
    1 pint strawberries, sliced, or 6 ounces cranberries
  ¼ cup orange juice
    1 teaspoon sugar
    2 pears, peeled and cubed
    2 Cortland or Granny Smith apples, peeled and cubed
    1 cup toasted pecan pieces or slivered almonds
1½ teaspoons kosher salt
    2 teaspoons black pepper
       pinch of ground allspice

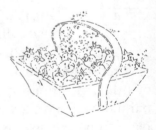

Cook Wild Rice according to recipe on page 179, but use ½ cup less water; set aside to cool.

Preheat oven to 350 degrees. Steep tea bag in 2 cups boiling water. In large bowl, soak raisins, prunes and apricots in sherry, tea and water to cover. Soak 1 hour.

Meanwhile, combine strawberries or cranberries, orange juice and sugar in food processor or blender. Use only a few on-off turns to break fruit into small pieces, then add to raisin mixture. Add pears and apples to the mixture, and soak 30 minutes longer. Add toasted nuts, salt, pepper, allspice and the cooked wild rice. Mix well and bake separately for 45 minutes in an ovenproof dish  covered with foil. Serve as an accompaniment with the goose.

BRAISED RED CABBAGE

SERVES
6

- 1 head red cabbage, about 1 to 1½ pounds
- 2 apples, peeled, cored and thinly sliced
- 1 cup sweet butter
- 2 tablespoons lemon juice
- ¾ cup white wine
- ½ teaspoon dry mustard
- 2 teaspoons kosher salt
- 1 teaspoon black pepper
- 1½ tablespoons caraway seeds

Quarter the cabbage, then shred and combine with apples.

Melt the butter in a large skillet; add lemon juice, wine, mustard, salt and pepper. Bring to boil. Add the cabbage and apples and cook over medium heat, covering skillet with aluminum foil to help steam, turning occasionally, until the cabbage is wilted and soft, about 15 minutes. Add caraway seeds and serve.

CREAMED PEARL ONIONS

YIELDS
3 CUPS

6 tablespoons sweet butter
2 pints pearl onions, peeled
½ teaspoon kosher salt
¼ teaspoon white pepper
½ cup dry sherry
1 cup chicken stock
2 cups heavy cream
1 scant tablespoon chopped fresh thyme or sage or chopped fresh parsley

Melt 4 tablespoons of the butter in a large skillet; add onions, salt and pepper, and sauté over medium-high heat about 15 minutes, stirring occasionally, until onions start to brown. Reduce heat and cook onions 20 minutes longer, until soft. Remove onions with slotted spoon to bowl.

Add the remaining 2 tablespoons butter to skillet; let it get brown, add sherry and reduce liquid to 1 tablespoon. Add stock and reduce mixture to 2 tablespoons. Add cream and scrape bottom of the skillet to deglaze. Cook about 5 minutes, until mixture is reduced enough to coat spoon. Add reserved onions and cook until mixture is reduced to 3 cups. Toss in thyme, sage or parsley. Correct seasonings.

Hanukkah

Hanukkah is the holiday commemorating the bravery of the Jewish people through the ages. It's a time of celebration and thanks for the familiar and basic joys of life.

✦✦✦✦✦✦✦✦✦✦✦✦✦✦✦✦✦✦✦✦✦✦✦✦✦✦✦✦✦✦✦✦✦✦

TZIMMES
(ROAST CHICKEN

with

PRUNES AND CARROTS)

✦

PECAN MOLASSES
ACORN SQUASH

✦

MASHED
POTATO PANCAKES

with

APPLE SAUCE

✦✦✦✦✦✦✦✦✦✦✦✦✦✦✦✦✦✦✦✦✦✦✦✦✦✦✦✦✦✦✦✦✦✦

SERVES   For this Jewish holiday, we always serve the traditional roast chicken—not so glamorous as
___8___   goose, but so delicious and homey, especially
with a honey marinade and accompanied by prunes and carrots. It tastes ever better the second day. Our side dishes are

variations on the traditional theme. As is customary to honor the ancients, oil is a key ingredient in any Hanukkah meal. We invented a fabulous sweet and crispy vegetable dish of double deep-fried acorn squash, cut to retain its natural scalloped outline and crusted with molasses and pecans. Instead of the traditional grated potato pancakes, we serve mashed potato pancakes with a side dish of apple sauce.

TZIMMES (ROAST CHICKEN WITH PRUNES AND CARROTS)

S E R V E S
8

2 three-pound roasting chickens, cleaned, cut in quarters
5 pounds carrots, peeled, halved lengthwise and cut in ½-inch slices
1 pound pitted prunes
1 pound dried apricots
½ cup honey
1 cup fresh orange juice
3 to 4 medium cloves garlic, minced
1 teaspoon kosher salt
1 teaspoon white pepper
1 cup soy sauce
1 cup white wine
2 teaspoons chopped fresh thyme

Combine all ingredients in a large bowl and let marinate 1 to 2 hours in refrigerator, if possible.

Preheat oven to 350 degrees.

Separate white from dark pieces of chicken, place in ovenproof dishes, and pour marinade over. Bake white meat 40 to 45 minutes, the dark 45 to 55 minutes.

PECAN MOLASSES ACORN SQUASH

vegetable oil or shortening for deep frying
3 medium acorn squash, halved, cleaned and cut in ½-inch slices

DRY MIX

1 cup all-purpose flour
1 tablespoon ground cinnamon
1 teaspoon ground allspice
1 teaspoon ground ginger
1 teaspoon kosher salt
1 teaspoon white pepper

PECAN MIX

2 cups coarsely chopped pecans
1 cup yellow cornmeal
1 teaspoon kosher salt

MOLASSES MIX

2 cups molasses
¼ cup maple syrup
½ cup bourbon
4 eggs, lightly beaten
1 teaspoon kosher salt

Preheat oil to 300 degrees in a deep-fryer. Line a bowl with paper towels. Fry the squash until soft, about 7 minutes, turning regularly. Do not crowd squash. When cooked, place in paper-towel-lined bowl.

Meanwhile, combine ingredients for dry mix in 1 bowl, molasses mix in another, pecan mix in a third.

Turn up heat under oil to 375 degrees.

With left hand, dip squash into the dry mix, then into molasses mix. With the right hand, dredge squash in pecan mix. This way your working hand does not get all sticky, and at the same time you can fry squash without washing your hands every few minutes.

Drop squash into hot oil about 6 pieces at a time, taking care not to crowd it, for then only the pecans will burn. Cook squash about 3 minutes, then remove to paper towel. Keep warm in the oven with chicken, or in a 200-degree oven if making squash separately.

MASHED POTATO PANCAKES

10 cups mashed potatoes (see page 112) about 6 pounds
 4 large eggs, lightly beaten
 1 cup bread crumbs
 1 teaspoon dry mustard
¼ cup chopped fresh parsley
   dash of cayenne
 1 teaspoon kosher salt
 1 teaspoon pepper
 1 cup vegetable oil

Combine potatoes, eggs, bread crumbs, mustard, parsley, cayenne, salt and pepper. Form into 3-inch ovals, using ¼ cup batter for each pancake.

Heat oil as needed in a large skillet; fry pancakes 4 minutes on each side, until golden and crisp. Keep warm in a 200-degee oven. Serve the pancakes, being kept warm, with a side dish of apple sauce.

APPLE SAUCE

½ cup brown sugar
¼ cup apple cider or water
 3 pounds apples (Cortland or Macintosh), peeled, cored, and cubed in 1-inch pieces
 2 teaspoons lemon juice
 1 teaspoon cinnamon
⅛ teaspoon cloves
½ cup golden raisins (optional)

Place sugar and water in saucepan. Stir until sugar is dissolved. Add remaining ingredients.

Cook over low heat for 20 minutes or until apples are soft. Remove from heat and stir rigorously until smooth (some apple chunks will remain). If using raisins, add after removing from heat.

New Year's Eve

We hate partying on New Year's Eve, preferring instead to stay in the restaurant and cook for friends and customers. Our special meal is costly and extravagant, and one for which we spend the entire year planning and testing recipes.

✳✳✳✳✳✳✳✳✳✳✳✳✳✳✳✳✳✳✳✳✳✳✳✳

FILET OF BEEF

with

PERNOD
BUTTER SAUCE

✳

SAUTÉED
SNOW PEAS

and

CHERRY TOMATOES

✳

GARLIC
POTATOES

✳✳✳✳✳✳✳✳✳✳✳✳✳✳✳✳✳✳✳✳✳✳✳✳

SERVES   We are just giving you the main course, but you can prepare a soup or appetizer, a wild salad, cheese platter and dessert. New Year's Eve is a time for stuffing yourself.

8

FILET OF BEEF

SERVES
8

1 whole beef filet, tied, or cut into 8 eight-ounce steaks
1 to 2 teaspoons kosher salt
1 to 2 teaspoons coarse black pepper
2 small cloves garlic, minced
4 tablespoons melted sweet butter
1 recipe Pernod Sauce (recipe follows)

Preheat oven to 350 degrees.

To prepare the whole filet, place it in a 12- by-18-inch roaster, then rub its surface with the salt, pepper and garlic, and then drizzle on the butter. Cook for 50 to 60 minutes for medium-rare meat. Baste every 15 minutes with pan drippings.

To prepare steaks, place them in the roaster and rub the surfaces with the salt, pepper, garlic, and then drizzle on the butter. Cook 7 to 8 minutes per side for medium-rare meat.

PERNOD BUTTER SAUCE

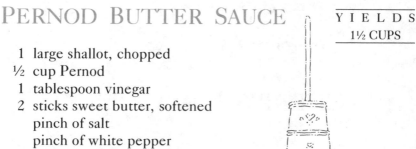

YIELDS
1½ CUPS

1 large shallot, chopped
½ cup Pernod
1 tablespoon vinegar
2 sticks sweet butter, softened
  pinch of salt
  pinch of white pepper
½ tablespoon chopped fresh parsley
¾ teaspoon roasted anise seeds

Place shallot, Pernod and vinegar in saucepan over low heat. Turn up heat a little, swirling pan so liquid evaporates evenly. Reduce until only 1 tablespoon liquid remains. Turn heat very low and whisk in small globs of butter, dropping them in with fingers, whisking constantly with other hand. So the pan will not move, block the pan with handle against your body, since you have no hand free to hold the pot. Whisk in each glob completely before dropping in the next. If it seems to get too hot, take off heat for a few seconds.

Remove from heat and add salt, pepper, parsley and anise seeds. Whisk and taste. Let sit for 10 minutes, then correct seasoning, if desired.

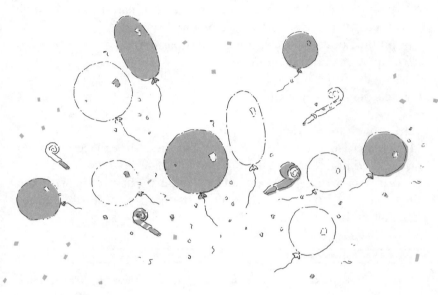

SAUTÉED SNOW PEAS AND CHERRY TOMATOES

SERVES
8

2 pounds snow peas, cleaned and blanched
4 tablespoons clarified butter, melted
1 box cherry tomatoes, washed, stems removed, and halved if large
   salt and pepper to taste
1 tablespoon fresh parsley

Go over the snow peas after they are blanched, making sure there are no blushes. When the rest of your dinner is almost ready, heat the butter in a *sautoir* (see glossary) over medium heat. Throw in the snow peas and 2 small cherry tomatoes per person. Sauté just enough to heat through, so that tomatoes retain their shape.

At the last minute, add a pinch of salt and pepper and the tablespoon of parsley.

GARLIC POTATOES

SERVES
8

 5 pounds new potatoes of uniform size, prepared tournée style
    in cold water to cover with a pinch of salt, or
 3 pounds new potatoes, unpeeled, quartered
 ⅔ cup sweet butter, melted
 3 cloves garlic, minced
1½ teaspoons kosher salt

Preheat oven to 375 degrees.

   If you are using tournéed potatoes, pat them dry. Place tournéed
or quartered potatoes on a baking sheet; add garlic to melted butter
and rub it onto the potatoes; and sprinkle them evenly with the
salt. Place in the oven and cook 30 to 40 minutes, or until potatoes
are a golden brown.

---

*A tournéed potato, with its 7 equal sides, is beautiful,
and, because all sides are even, it cooks uniformly. It
would add a special touch to the Garlic Potatoes or a
similar recipe. But be prepared to practice before you
perfect this 2-handed movement. Hold the potato in one
hand, and with the paring knife in the other, trim off
each end, then cut off slices to make 7 equal faces, or
surfaces. Rotate the potato after each cut. Put the tournéed potatoes into a bowl of cold water with a pinch of
salt. This prevents them from turning brown before cooking. If you are using tournéed potatoes, more will be
needed because of loss of skin.*

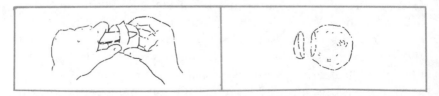

St. Patrick's Day

✸✸✸✸✸✸✸✸✸✸✸✸✸✸✸✸✸✸✸✸✸✸✸✸✸✸✸✸✸✸✸✸✸

NEW ENGLAND BOILED DINNER

✸

IRISH SODA BREAD

✸

MUSTARD HORSERADISH SAUCE

✸✸✸✸✸✸✸✸✸✸✸✸✸✸✸✸✸✸✸✸✸✸✸✸✸✸✸✸✸✸✸✸✸

SERVES

10

For the wearin' o' the Green, a traditional home-cooked meal to recall a bit of the old sod. This is super easy—everyone can pitch in to help, and there will be few pots to clean up. Also, there's plenty to eat, with maybe enough for leftovers for the non-Irish March 18 supper.

NEW ENGLAND BOILED DINNER

    10-pound corned beef brisket
  1 rutabaga, about 2 pounds, peeled and chunked
  4 white turnips, peeled and chunked
10 carrots, peeled and chunked
10 parsnips, peeled and chunked
20 new potatoes, scrubbed and halved
  2 heads cabbage, about 5 pounds total
     chopped parsley for garnish
     Mustard Horseradish Sauce (recipe on page 210)
     coarse-grained mustard

Put corned beef in large pot with water to cover. Bring to a boil. Reduce heat and simmer, uncovered, 1 hour. Add rutabaga. Cook 30 minutes longer, then add white turnips, carrots, parsnips and potatoes. Cook, uncovered, 1½ to 2 hours longer.

    Meanwhile, bring another pot of water to a boil. Cut cabbages into 3-inch wedges. Place in boiling water and cook 10 to 12 minutes. Remove corned beef from water; let stand 10 minutes. Slice meat against the grain. Drain vegetables, and arrange corned beef and vegetables on large platter. Sprinkle with chopped parsley. Serve with Mustard Horseradish Sauce and coarse-grained mustard.

IRISH SODA BREAD

  2 cups all-purpose flour
  1 teaspoon baking soda
½ teaspoon salt
  2 tablespoons sugar
½ cup butter, softened
½ cup golden raisins
  1 tablespoon caraway seeds
     grated zest of 1 lemon
½ cup buttermilk
  1 egg mixed with 1 tablespoon water

Preheat oven to 350 degrees. Lightly grease baking sheet.

In a large bowl combine the flour, baking soda, salt and sugar. Cut in butter until mixture is the size of peas. Stir in the raisins, caraway seeds and lemon zest. Add the buttermilk, mixing and kneading lightly into a ball. Place on the baking sheet and shape into a domed round loaf. With a sharp knife, make a large cross on top, extending from side to side. Brush with egg wash. Bake 45 minutes, or until evenly golden on top and bottom.

MUSTARD HORSERADISH SAUCE

YIELDS
2 CUPS

⅓ cup heavy cream
3 tablespoons Dijon mustard
2 tablespoons prepared white horseradish
½ teaspoon kosher salt
½ teaspoon ground white pepper
½ cup sour cream, at room temperature
2 teaspoons lemon juice
2 tablespoons olive oil

Whisk cream in dry bowl with dry whisk until it holds soft peaks. Whisk in mustard, horseradish, salt and pepper. Whisk in sour cream and lemon juice. Drizzle in oil, whisking constantly.

Easter

Easter is one of the most joyous holidays of the year. Its religious significance promises new life and is complemented by nature's growing strength after the long winter. Our Easter dinner highlights this spring mood.

✼✼✼✼✼✼✼✼✼✼✼✼✼✼✼✼✼✼✼✼✼✼✼✼✼✼✼✼✼✼✼✼✼✼✼✼

BAKED
GLAZED HAM

✼

SWEET POTATOES
DAUPHINOISE

✼

SAUTÉED ASPARAGUS

✼

STRAWBERRY
and
RHUBARB RELISH

✼✼✼✼✼✼✼✼✼✼✼✼✼✼✼✼✼✼✼✼✼✼✼✼✼✼✼✼✼✼✼✼✼✼✼✼

S E R V E S   Such a celebratory day obviously merits feast foods. Traditionally, cooks serve baked ham or roast lamb, spring vegetables such as asparagus and new potatoes, and a rich dessert to break Lent's long fast. At Good Enough to Eat, we observe the holiday with this special dinner.

10

BAKED GLAZED HAM

SERVES
10

18- to 20-pound cured ham, bone in
1½ cups apricot jam
1½ cups Grand Marnier or Triple Sec
1 cup dark raisins
3 juice oranges sliced very thin, plus 1 orange halved
whole cloves

Preheat oven to 350 degrees.

Remove all but ¼-inch fat from ham with knife. Then make crisscross markings over the remaining fat. Place ham in an 18- by-24-inch roasting pan. Spread ham with jam.

In a small pan combine liqueur with raisins; simmer 10 minutes, then remove from heat and let raisins steep in liqueur 30 minutes.

Stick orange slices to the ham with the cloves, piercing the oranges through their center. If some fall into the pan, don't worry. Squeeze remaining orange halves over the ham and add them to the roasting pan.

Bake ham 50 minutes, then pour liqueur and raisins over it. Bake 30 minutes longer, basting the ham every 15 minutes.

SWEET POTATOES DAUPHINOISE

SERVES
10

5½ pounds sweet potatoes, peeled and sliced very thin
1 cup butter, softened
¼ pound Parmesan cheese, grated
1 large onion, halved and sliced very thin
3 large cloves garlic, minced
4 cups heavy cream
1 cup milk
¼ teaspoon ground cinnamon
¼ teaspoon ground nutmeg
2 tablespoons kosher salt
1 teaspoon ground white pepper

Preheat oven to 350 degrees. *(continued on next page)*

Peel and slice the potatoes very thin, taking care to make every slice uniform and to remove all the blemishes. Rub an 18- by-12-inch baking pan with ¼ of the butter. Sprinkle all over with ¼ of the Parmesan. Then place one third of sweet potatoes in rows, overlapping slightly. Layer on ⅓ of the onion slices, garlic, butter, cream, milk and Parmesan; combine the cinnamon, nutmeg, kosher salt and pepper and sprinkle ⅓ of mixture onto layer. Repeat twice, with the last layer of potatoes (3rd layer) overlapping in rows like fish scales; top with remaining butter and Parmesan.

Bake, covered with foil, for 30 minutes. Uncover and bake 15 to 30 minutes longer, until a knife inserted in center comes out easily.

SAUTÉED ASPARAGUS

SERVES
10

5	pounds asparagus (allow 5 spears per person)
1½	teaspoons kosher salt
5	tablespoons lemon juice (reserve the squeezed lemon)
3	hard-cooked eggs
8	tablespoons sweet butter
¼	cup fresh parsley
1	teaspoon white pepper

✶✶

When selecting asparagus, look for firm, unblemished stalks with tight tips. To prepare, cut off the tough white end of each stalk. Then hold the stalk by its head in one hand, resting its base on the table. With a potato peeler held in the other hand, peel the stalk from its midpoint to its base. Make each stalk as smooth and round as possible.

✶✶

Place enough water to cover asparagus in a large pot. Bring to boil with 1 teaspoon salt, 3 tablespoons lemon juice and the squeezed lemon. Place asparagus in water; bring back to a boil. Reduce heat and simmer 4 to 5 minutes, depending on thickness of asparagus. Shock under cold water as soon as asparagus are done.

Cut eggs in half; separate yolks from whites. Separately sieve whites and yolks. Using a wooden spoon, push the ingredients through the sieve. Mix with the parsley; set aside.

Combine half the butter with 1½ tablespoons lemon juice, and ½ teaspoon salt and pepper over medium heat. Add half the asparagus and sauté a few minutes, until heated through. Reduce the liquid by half. Remove from pan to serving dish and sprinkle ½ the egg mix over center of the asparagus. Drizzle with the butter sauce. Repeat with remaining half.

STRAWBERRY AND RHUBARB RELISH

YIELDS
3 CUPS

  ½ cup fresh orange juice
  ¼ cup lemon juice
   1 cup firmly packed dark brown sugar
  ½ teaspoon ground cinnamon
   1 pint ripe strawberries, washed, stems removed, halved if large
1¾ pounds rhubarb, cleaned and cut in 1-inch cubes

Place orange juice, lemon juice, sugar and cinnamon in a small saucepan over low heat. Swirl, do not stir, until sugar is dissolved. Simmer 10 minutes. Add strawberries and rhubarb. Bring to a boil, then reduce to a simmer and cook 20 to 30 minutes, or until fruit is very soft. Correct seasoning. If the fruit is too watery, remove it with slotted spoon, reduce liquid to a syrup and pour it over the fruit.

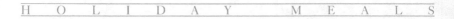

Mother's Day

✸✸✸✸✸✸✸✸✸✸✸✸✸✸✸✸✸✸✸✸✸✸✸✸

BAKED
LAMB CHOPS

with

ORANGE
CREAM SAUCE

✸

POTATO–STRING
BEAN SALAD

✸✸✸✸✸✸✸✸✸✸✸✸✸✸✸✸✸✸✸✸✸✸✸✸

S E R V E S   We all dote on Mom! And what better way to show her our love and appreciation than to pre- pare her an elegantly simple dinner. We suggest this springtime meal of lamb chops baked with an orange cream sauce and accompanied by a potato and string bean salad. This is so easy that even children can prepare it. Remember to make the salad at least 1 hour in advance. This salad does not make good leftovers because the potatoes discolor.

8

BAKED LAMB CHOPS

SERVES
8

16 three-quarter-inch-thick lamb chops
½ cup olive oil
2 cloves garlic
1½ teaspoons dried basil
1½ teaspoons dried thyme
  pinch of salt
  pinch of pepper
  Orange Cream Sauce (recipe follows)

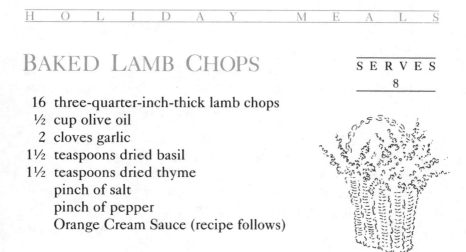

Preheat oven to 375 degrees.

Heat oil and garlic in a small saucepan for 5 minutes. Add basil, thyme, salt and pepper. Remove from heat and let sit for 20 minutes to allow flavor to develop.

Brush oil on both sides of the lamb chops. Place on baking sheet and bake 6 to 7 minutes on each side. Cut into chop near the bone to see if it is done enough for you. Press gently with your finger to learn exactly how it feels, so you can tell without cutting it next time.

The chops can also be broiled or grilled.

ORANGE CREAM SAUCE

YIELDS
2 CUPS

1 cup sweet butter
½ teaspoon kosher salt
½ teaspoon white pepper
¼ teaspoon cayenne
1 cup white wine
2 cups freshly squeezed orange juice
1 teaspoon grated orange zest
1 teaspoon lemon juice
3 cups heavy cream
  julienned zest of half an orange

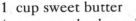

(continued on next page)

Melt butter with salt, pepper and cayenne over low heat, being careful not to let the butter burn. Add the wine and reduce the liquid by one quarter. Whisk in the orange juice, grated zest, and lemon juice. Cook 1 minute. Remove from heat and whisk in cream. Return to stove and over medium heat reduce the liquid by half, whisking constantly. Add the julienned orange zest. For julienned orange zest, peel off orange zest, then turn zest over and saw off the white part (pith). Julienne as thinly as possible. Dip in boiling water for 3 seconds to soften and remove bitter taste.

This is a very rich sauce; serve 2 tablespoons each lamb chop. Bring the rest to the table in a sauceboat.

POTATO–STRING BEAN SALAD

SERVES
8

DRESSING

    2 cups vegetable oil
    1 cup chopped walnuts
    ⅓ cup freshly squeezed lemon juice
      grated rind of one lemon
    2 teaspoons kosher salt
    1½ teaspoons white pepper
      pinch of cayenne
    1 tablespoon chopped fresh tarragon (optional)
    3 pounds small new potatoes, cooked and cut into bite-sized
      pieces
    2 pounds green beans, cut 3 inches long, blanched 2 minutes

In a small saucepan heat oil; add walnuts and cook over very low heat 15 minutes. Remove from heat and let sit 10 minutes longer. Stir in lemon juice, lemon rind, salt, pepper, cayenne and tarragon (if desired).

Place potatoes and string beans in a large bowl. Add dressing and mix.

Father's Day

****

BRISKET OF BEEF

*

NOODLE PUDDING

****

SERVES Dad deserves his day, too, and so that he won't feel neglected, prepare him this delicious, ro-**10 TO 12** bust dinner of brisket of beef and noodle pudding. No hunger pangs here.

****

Searing meat browns it quickly in very hot oil and is ideal for sealing in juices in tougher cuts of meats. Searing also gives meat a crunchy texture, a browned surface and a heartier taste. Coat meat pieces in seasoned flour first, and sear in half oil-half butter mixture. Sear only a few pieces at a time, or the oil temperature will lower and the meat will stew. After searing, add some wine or water and deglaze (see page 101) the pan to capture all the juices and crusty pieces of fat and meat.

****

BRISKET OF BEEF

    9- to 11-pound brisket of beef
½ cup all-purpose flour seasoned with 2 teaspoons kosher salt
    and 1 teaspoon ground black pepper
¼ cup olive oil
2 large onions, sliced ¼ inch thick
2 cloves garlic, minced
4 stalks celery, chopped
2 pounds carrots, chunked
1 dozen new potatoes, peeled
2 cups canned plum tomatoes, crushed with hand
1½ cups canned crushed tomatoes
1½ cups beef stock
1 cup red wine
2 tablespoons chopped fresh thyme or 2 teaspoons dried
½ teaspoon dried basil
1 tablespoon kosher salt
1 teaspoon ground black pepper
¼ cup chopped fresh parsley

Preheat oven to 325 degrees.

    Coat meat with flour. Pour oil in an 18-by-24-inch roasting pan and heat. Sear brisket on all sides; remove meat from pan, leaving oil.

    Add onions to pan and brown for 5 minutes. Add garlic and sauté, scraping pan regularly, until garlic is soft. Place meat back into pan. Surround with celery, carrots, and potatoes. Add remaining ingredients except parsley. Cover with foil and roast in oven for 2 hours. Add parsley; uncover and roast 45 to 55 minutes longer.

NOODLE PUDDING

SERVES
10 TO 12

2 pounds extra-wide egg noodles
1 tablespoon olive oil
4 large eggs, slightly beaten
2 cups sour cream
2 cups cottage cheese
¼ pound cream cheese, softened
1 cup raisins, preferably golden
¼ cup apricot or peach preserves
1 teaspoon kosher salt
½ teaspoon white pepper
1 tablespoon sugar combined with ½ teaspoon ground cinnamon
4 tablespoons sweet butter, softened

Preheat oven to 350 degrees. Grease 18-by-12-inch baking dish.

Cook noodles *al dente* in stockpot according to package directions. Drain, rinse and place in a large bowl. Toss with olive oil.

In a separate bowl, combine the eggs, sour cream, cottage cheese, cream cheese, raisins, preserves, salt and pepper until well blended; combine with noodles, mixing well. Add mixture to baking dish, sprinkle with cinnamon-sugar and dot with butter. Bake 40 minutes.

5

DESSERTS

mericans have a particular passion for desserts—more so, we'd say, than any other nationality does. In Europe, for instance, a pastry is reserved for a very special Sunday treat; here, few main meals end without some tempting baked goody. Our national sweet tooth prompts us to daydream about desserts and to indulge in an endless quest for the ideal cake, pie or cookie. Certainly, many home cooks pride themselves more on baking beautiful cakes than on serving perfectly fried chicken. And just consider all the baking contests, bake sales and bake-offs we hold in every town and for every imaginable event. What's more,

don't we all feel that a neatly wrapped bundle of brownies or a wedge of freshly baked cake is a thoughtful house present or an appropriate consolation for a sick friend? As a result, almost all of us equate some dessert or baked goods with love and caring.

We have approached baked desserts at Good Enough to Eat in that same spirit. We want to satiate, pamper and please our customers like family members. Therefore we don't prepare the elegant, tricky pastries so often served in restaurants. Instead, our desserts are familiar and homey, reminding our customers of treasured childhood tastes: towering chocolate cakes smeared with fudgy frosting, flaky pies bulging with spiced fruit, gently sweetened crunchy cookies that taste so good with milk. Yet our desserts are appealing and attractive, so we display them on counters right  up front. These are what people see first when they walk through our doors. And every portion we serve is oversized—would a mother be skimpy?

Nowhere else in the world do people go as mad for fruit pies as in America. They are the quintessential American dessert. When we carry a freshly baked fruit pie through either of our restaurants to our front display counter, everyone gasps with delight at the fragrance of spiced fruit and flaky pastry just out of the oven. We usually serve these pies warm with whipped cream or ice cream.

After much work and baking, we have developed what we think is the perfect pie crust. (For the recipe, see page 224.) Most importantly, we urge you to use very cold butter and very cold water so the gluten in the flour will not react and the dough become tough. Use whatever utensils you wish—knives, forks, pastry cutters or fingers, if you feel confident—to cut the butter into the flour, until the mixture resembles peas in size. If you use your fingers, rub the flour/butter through them quickly, brushing your thumb against your fingertips, starting with your little finger. Add the water in a steady stream into the flour/butter and use a fork to stir the water in, but use your hands to bring the dough together into a ball. Never knead pie dough because that causes the gluten to react with the flour and to toughen the crust. Wrap the dough in plastic and refrigerate for at least half an hour. This gives the dough time to relax and to let the butter firm up again. Keeping the butter cold causes it to take that much longer to melt once the crust is in the oven, and this will produce a flakier crust.

With a lightly floured rolling pin, roll out the dough on a lightly floured surface, working always only in one direction, moving the dough around to form a circle. Never rest your rolling pin on the dough because that affects texture. You'll know your crust has the ideal texture if you see little clumps of butter as you roll out the dough. Flip the dough over once to prevent its sticking, and reflour the surface. Fold the dough circle in half, and ease into the pie tin. Unfold, crimp the edges, then place the shell in the refrigerator to relax again.

Because we love juicy, gooey pies, we never use fillers, except flour, as binding agents. To assure nonsoggy crusts, brush a glaze of jam heated with a little lemon juice on the bottom crust before adding the filling. To make a golden top crust, brush an egg-and-water wash on top; for a browner, crunchier crust, sprinkle sugar on the wash.

Pies

BASIC PIECRUST RECIPE

1½ cups all-purpose flour
½ cup very cold sweet butter
¼ cup ice-cold water

YIELDS
2
NINE-INCH
CRUSTS

Place flour in a bowl. Cut in pieces of butter with a pastry blender or 2 knives until mixture resembles peas. Add water gradually, using a fork to gather the dough (you may use your hands if you work quickly so as not to warm the butter). Use only as much water as needed to form the dough into a self-clinging ball. Divide in 2. Wrap in plastic and refrigerate at least 30 minutes, until firm.

When ready to make piecrust, lightly flour the rolling pin and pastry board. Press down on one ball of dough with the rolling pin. Starting at the center, roll out dough in circle in only one direction at a time, first to the top, then to the sides, then to the bottom. Do not roll back to the center. Flip the dough over once so it does not stick to the board.

When dough is desired size (about 10 inches around), fold it in half and slide it into the pie plate. Unfold dough, trim, and if you are making a 1-crust pie, crimp the edges.

Refrigerate for 30 minutes longer to allow the dough to relax. Wrap remaining dough in foil, date the package, and freeze for up to 2 months.

If making a 2-crust pie, do not crimp edges of bottom crust. When bottom crust is filled, roll out second half of dough, moisten edges of bottom crust, place second crust over filling, and fold edges of the top crust under the bottom crust. Crimp edges with fork or finger to seal.

MOM'S APPLE PIE

dough for 2 nine-inch pastry shells (Piecrust recipe on page 224)
8 Cortland or Macintosh apples
¼ cup all-purpose flour
½ to ¾ cup sugar plus 1 tablespoon
1 tablespoon ground cinnamon
⅛ teaspoon ground allspice
juice of 1 lemon
grated rind of 1 lemon
3 tablespoons sweet butter
1 large egg beaten with 1 tablespoon water

Preheat the oven to 375 degrees.

Roll out half of the dough to fit 9-inch pie plate, leaving ½ inch overhang. Refrigerate until ready to fill.

Peel, core, and slice the apples into a mixing bowl. Add the flour, ½ to ¾ cup sugar, depending on tartness of apples, the cinnamon, allspice, lemon juice and lemon rind. Toss the mixture, place it in the prepared pastry shell, and dot with butter. Moisten edges of bottom crust with cold butter.

Roll out remaining half of dough to a 10-inch circle and place it over the apples. Tuck the top crust under the bottom crust and crimp the edges. With a knife, make several vents on top. Brush the crust with egg wash and sprinkle it with the remaining table-spoon sugar.

Bake 15 minutes. Reduce temperature to 350 degrees, and bake the pie 30 minutes longer, until the crust is golden brown and the filling is bubbling lightly.

PEAR AND GINGER PIE

SERVES
6 TO 8

- 8 pears, peeled, cored and thinly sliced
- ¼ cup all-purpose flour
- ½ cup sugar
- 2 teaspoons ground ginger
- 2 tablespoons lemon juice
- 9-inch pastry shell, chilled (recipe on page 224)

TOPPING

- 1 cup confectioner's sugar
- 1 cup all-purpose flour
- ½ cup sweet butter, melted and slightly cooled
- ¼ teaspoon ground cinnamon

Preheat the oven to 375 degrees.

Combine the pears with the flour, sugar, ginger and lemon juice. Toss to coat the pears well; set aside.

To make the topping combine the confectioner's sugar with the flour, butter and cinnamon, stirring until the mixture is crumbly.

Place the pear mixture in the pastry shell. Spread the topping over the pears. Bake 15 minutes. Lower temperature to 300 and bake 30 minutes longer.

Like the British, we always use dark brown sugar because it helps assure moist cakes, and the richer taste that we love in our foods. To prevent hardening, store brown sugar with a piece of apple, pear or bread.

SOUR CREAM PEACH AND BLUEBERRY PIE

SERVES
6 TO 8

dough for 9-inch pastry
shell, chilled (page 224)
1½ cups sour cream
2 extra-large eggs
¼ cup all-purpose flour
1 cup sugar
1 teaspoon vanilla extract
½ teaspoon ground cinnamon
grated rind of 1 lemon
3 fresh peaches, peeled and sliced in ¼-inch wedges
2½ cups blueberries

TOPPING

¾ cup firmly packed brown
sugar
½ cup all-purpose flour
2 teaspoons ground cinnamon
½ cup walnut pieces
½ cup sweet butter, softened

Roll out dough to fit 9-inch pie plate; trim; crimp edges. Refrigerate until ready to fill.

Preheat oven to 375 degrees.

In a large bowl, combine the sour cream, eggs, flour, sugar, vanilla extract, cinnamon and lemon rind. Add the peaches and blueberries. Stir gently only until fruit is well coated; overstirring will cause the blueberries to bleed. Pour the mixture into the pastry shell. Place the pie plate on a cookie sheet to catch drips during baking. Bake 30 to 35 minutes, or until the crust is lightly browned and custard is set.

Meanwhile, to make the topping combine all ingredients except the butter. Cut in the butter with a pastry blender or 2 knives until the mixture is slightly moist, but not a soft ball. Do not overwork dough or the butter will melt and run during baking.

When custard is set and beige in color, sprinkle topping mixture evenly over the pie. Return the pie to the oven to bake another 12 to 15 minutes or until topping is light brown.

APRICOT CRUMBLE PIE

SERVES
6 TO 8

3 pounds fresh apricots
2 extra-large eggs, lightly
  beaten
¼ cup all-purpose flour
½ cup sugar
1 teaspoon almond extract
  9-inch pastry shell, chilled
  (page 224)

TOPPING

1½ cups all-purpose flour
½ cup sugar
½ cup sweet butter,
  softened
1½ cups slivered almonds
1 teaspoon almond extract

Preheat oven to 350 degrees.

Bring saucepan of water to boil. Drop apricots in boiling water for 8 to 10 seconds; remove, peel, halve and discard pits. (You should have about 4 cups apricot halves.)

Combine the eggs, ¼ cup flour, ½ cup sugar and 1 teaspoon almond extract in a bowl. Fold in apricots and set aside.

To make the topping combine the 1½ cups flour and ½ cup sugar. Cut in the butter until the mixture is the size of peas, then stir in the almonds and 1 teaspoon almond extract.

Place the apricot mixture in the pastry shell. Crumble the topping mixture evenly over the apricot mixture. Bake the pie 40 to 45 minutes, or until the fruit is soft and topping is browned.

APPLE BROWN BETTY

SERVES
8

A truly basic New England fall dessert. For this crustless pie, you can use slightly overripe apples, if you wish, because the slices don't have to keep their shape. When all the ingredients bake together, this dessert resembles a bread pudding.

6 tart apples, peeled, cored and thinly sliced
1 teaspoon ground cinnamon
¼ teaspoon ground nutmeg
½ cup firmly packed brown sugar
¼ cup honey
¼ cup golden raisins

24 graham crackers, crushed (1 cup crumbs)
¼ cup sweet butter, melted, plus ¼ cup
½ cup walnut pieces
½ cup apple cider
    ice cream or heavy cream

Preheat oven to 350 degrees.

Combine apples with the cinnamon, nutmeg, sugar, honey and raisins; set aside.

In a separate bowl, combine the graham cracker crumbs with ¼ cup of the melted butter and the walnut pieces; sprinkle ⅓ of the mixture over the bottom of a 9-inch baking dish. Top with half the apple mixture, then pour over half the apple cider. Layer in ⅓ of the crumbs, the remaining apple mixture, cider, and the last ⅓ of crumbs. Dot with the remaining ¼ cup of butter. Cover with aluminum foil.

Bake 40 to 45 minutes, or until bubbly. Serve warm with ice cream or heavy cream.

CRANBERRY ORANGE CRISP

SERVES

6

*S*o easy to assemble, a child can whip it up. Use any seasonal fruit you have on hand, and serve the crisp with mounds of ice cream or a generous portion of heavy cream.

FILLING

3 cups fresh or frozen
    cranberries
    rind of 2 oranges, grated
¼ cup sugar
1 teaspoon cinnamon,
    ground

TOPPING

1½ cups all-purpose flour
1½ cups sugar
1½ teaspoons baking powder
¾ cup sweet butter, cut in ½"
    square pieces
1 large egg

Preheat the oven to 350 degrees.

Combine all the filling ingredients in a large mixing bowl. Place the mixture in a 9-by-12-inch baking pan and set aside.

For the topping, combine the flour, sugar and baking powder, then cut in the butter, but don't overwork. The butter should remain in small clomps. Stir in the egg. The topping should remain very crumbly. Mound the topping on the filling, and bake the crisp for 40 minutes. Serve warm.

LEMON MERINGUE PIE WITH CHOCOLATE GRAHAM CRUST

SERVES 8

O ne afternoon we sat around with some of our bakers and talked ourselves through this pie, step by step. It's a fascinating combination of flavors, some unexpected, yet the overall result is pure lemon meringue pie—a slightly tart custard filling crowned with a billowy meringue.

CHOCOLATE GRAHAM CRACKER CRUST

⅓ cup sweet butter, melted
1⅓ cups graham cracker crumbs
2 ounces sweet chocolate
¼ cup brown sugar

MERINGUE

6 egg whites
¼ teaspoon cream of tartar
12 tablespoons sugar

CUSTARD

1 cup sugar
2 tablespoons all-purpose flour
4 tablespoons cornstarch
¼ teaspoon salt
2 cups boiling water
3 large egg yolks
juice of 3 lemons
rind of 3 lemons, grated
1 tablespoon sweet butter
1 whole lemon
2 tablespoons raspberry jam

Preheat the oven to 350 degrees.

Melt the ⅓ cup of butter for the crust in a saucepan and set aside.

To prepare the crust, place the graham cracker crumbs in a large mixing bowl and, using the large holes of a grater, grate the chocolate right onto the crumbs. Add the sugar and melted butter and combine all ingredients. Pat them evenly into a 9-inch pie plate, pushing the crumbs ½ inch up the sides. Bake for 10 to 15 minutes, or until set and slightly brown.

While the crust bakes, begin to prepare the custard. Combine the sugar, flour, cornstarch and salt in a saucepan. Add the 2 cups boiling water and cook over low-medium heat, stirring vigorously with a wooden spoon until mixture begins to thicken. Continue to cook and stir until the mixture is thick. To warm up, or temper, the egg yolks, stir some heated mixture into them, then add the eggs to the saucepan. Add the lemon juice (reserving 1 tablespoon) and the rind, and continue cooking for another 3 minutes. Remove from the heat, add 1 tablespoon butter and stir until smooth. Let custard cool slightly.

While it cools, slice the whole lemon into paper-thin slices with a sharp, serrated fruit knife. Lay these slices on the crust to keep the crust from getting soggy. Soften the jam with the reserved lemon juice over low heat, then brush the lemon slices with the jam to seal in the lemon juice and keep the slices soft. It also adds an attractive dash of red. Pour the custard into the shell.

To make the meringue, put the eggs whites into a very clean, very dry bowl. Start to whip them with a whisk or electric mixer. When they are frothy, add the cream of tartar, then gradually add the sugar, about 1 tablespoon at a time. Continue beating until the whites form very stiff peaks. Mound them onto the pie custard, using a spoon to make high peaks. Place the pie back in the oven for 5 minutes, or until the meringue begins to brown. Cool completely before serving.

We love fluffy but moist cakes, so all ours contain sour cream or buttermilk, plus other liquids. We also like them high and majestic, with as many layers as possible.

We offer several hints for perfect cakes. First, all the ingredients must be at room temperature. Then prepare your cake pans. Cut out parchment paper circles to fit the bottom of the pans, or butter (with melted butter) and flour the pans well, banging the sides and turning the pans to distribute the flour evenly and to get rid of any clumps that might show up in the cake layer bottom. If you wish, use cocoa powder for "flouring" if you are making a chocolate cake.

Cream the butter with the sugar until light, fluffy, whitish, and without any lumps. If you see no color change, you have not beaten long enough. While beating, keep scraping down the sides of the bowl to incorporate everything. Finally, when combining wet with dry ingredients always alternate them, folding them in at slow speed. Start with the dry, add the wet, then the dry, then the wet, and finish with the last portion of the dry. To prevent crusty, dry cakes, never overbeat the batter once the flour is added.

If adding beaten egg whites separately, never, ever, overbeat them. The egg whites should be only as thick or stiff as the batter itself. After beating the whites to soft peaks, first stir in a large spoonful to the batter to expand it. Then fold in the rest of the whites with a large spoon that has a sharp cutting edge. You actually cut the whites in by making a figure 8 stirring motion until they are all incorporated.

If using melted chocolate in your cake batter, try to use top-quality chocolate such as the Belgian baking chocolate available at specialty-food stores. It's worth the extra money. Before melting it, cut big chunks into smaller ones so the chocolate melts uniformly and does not overcook. Melt chocolate in a microwave, a double boiler, or a bain-marie (see glossary), with the chocolate well up over the water so it doesn't scorch while melting. Stir regularly with a rubber spatula rather than a wooden spoon, which will absorb the chocolate. Chocolate is delicate and needs special treatment. Once it has been overcooked, you can't revive it. It tastes bitter and loses its shine. Cool the warm chocolate to room temperature before adding it to the batter. When adding the chocolate, never overstir, or the chocolate loses its shine and becomes crusty.

One final note: Work with cake ingredients in the following order. Cream the butter and sugar. Add the eggs and vanilla. Then add the melted chocolate. Then, alternate the dry with the wet ingredients. Finally, fold in the beaten whites.

To test for doneness: Use a toothpick or knife blade, stick it into the center of the cake and, if it comes out clean, the cake is done. With fudgy cakes, however, your toothpick or knife will have moist dough and cooked crumbs clinging to it.

Cakes

DEVIL'S FOOD CHOCOLATE CAKE

SERVES
10 TO 12

We share the concept of what a chocolate cake should be, and we spent nearly three years re-creating the exact taste from our collective childhood memory. This cake is moist and super-dark, and the frosting is fudgy. For extra flavor, we dust the frosted cake with unsweetened cocoa.

½ cup sweet butter, plus butter for
   preparing pans
1¾ cups brown sugar
 3 extra-large eggs
 2 tablespoons vanilla extract
 4 ounces unsweetened chocolate,
   melted and cooled to room
   temperature

2½ cups all-purpose flour
 2 teaspoons baking soda
 ½ teaspoon salt
1½ cups sour cream
1½ cups boiling water

Preheat the oven to 350 degrees.

Prepare 2 nine-inch layer cake pans by buttering them and dusting them with flour. In a large mixing bowl, cream the butter and sugar together until light and fluffy. Add the eggs, 1 at a time, beating well after each addition. Add the vanilla and cooled chocolate, mixing well. Combine the dry ingredients in a separate bowl, stirring together well. With the mixer at low speed, and scraping the bowl often with a rubber spatula, add the dry ingredients along with the sour cream, a few tablespoons at a time. Once combined, beat in the boiling water, mixing well. Immediately pour the batter into the prepared cake pans because the water makes the leavening agents react right away. Place the pans in the oven and bake for 20 to 25 minutes. Remove from the oven and cool slightly. Turn out the layers and cool completely on racks before frosting with Chocolate Frosting (recipe follows).

(Note: Chocolate lovers may want an even more intensely choc-
olate-flavored cake. If so, sprinkle ½ cup of sweetened chocolate
bits over each layer just before baking.)

CHOCOLATE FROSTING

1 pound cream cheese, softened	½ teaspoon freshly
¾ cup sweet butter, softened	squeezed lemon juice
4 cups unsifted confectioner's sugar	½ cup cocoa powder
½ teaspoon vanilla extract	

Start with the cream cheese and butter at room temperature, otherwise the frosting will be lumpy. Place butter in a large mixing
bowl and, with a hand or electric beater, beat until smooth. Add
cream cheese and cream them together well. Add the sugar slowly,
beating until smooth. Add the vanilla, lemon juice and cocoa powder and beat until thoroughly blended.

YELLOW CAKE

**SERVES
10 TO 12—
YIELDS
2 NINE-INCH
LAYERS**

A s with the chocolate cake, we
searched for the recipe that dupli-
cated the dense yellow cakes of our childhood, something that was finger-licking
delicious. We add buttermilk to our cake
to assure that it remains moist for several days.

1 cup sweet butter, softened	½ teaspoon baking soda
2 cups sugar	1 teaspoon plus pinch of salt
4 extra-large eggs, separated	1 cup buttermilk
1 teaspoon vanilla extract	Cream Cheese Frosting
2½ cups all-purpose flour	(page 242)
1 teaspoon baking powder	

Preheat the oven to 350 degrees. Grease and flour 2 nine-inch
round cake pans.

Cream the butter and sugar in a mixing bowl until light and
fluffy. Add the yolks 1 at a time, beating well after each addition.
Beat in the vanilla extract.

In a separate bowl, sift the flour, baking powder, baking soda and 1 teaspoon salt. Beat the dry ingredients into the butter-sugar mixture alternately with the buttermilk, ending with the dry ingredients. Clean the beaters thoroughly.

In a glass or stainless steel bowl (do not use plastic or aluminum), beat the egg whites with a pinch of salt until stiff but not dry. Fold ¼ of the whites into the batter, then fold in the remaining whites. Divide the batter between the pans.

Bake 20 to 25 minutes, or until tops are golden and a toothpick inserted in the centers comes out clean. Cool in the pans 10 minutes, then turn out onto wire racks to cool completely. Frost the cake with a cake-frosting knife on top and sides, using swirling motions.

LEMON YOGURT CAKE

SERVES
10 TO 12

*T*his rich but not oversweet cake resembles a pound cake. For a special treat, serve slices of it topped with fresh berries.

```
   1  cup plus 2 tablespoons sweet butter
2¾  cups plus 2 tablespoons all-purpose flour
   ½  teaspoon salt
   ½  teaspoon baking soda
   3  cups sugar
   5  extra-large eggs
   1  teaspoon vanilla extract
   1  cup plain yogurt
       grated zest of one lemon
   ¼  cup freshly squeezed lemon juice
```

Preheat the oven to 350 degrees.

Prepare a 10-inch Bundt pan by buttering it with the 2 tablespoons butter, and dust it with the 2 tablespoons of flour, knocking out any extra flour that might accumulate on the rounded pan bottom.

Combine the 2¾ cups flour and the baking soda and salt in a mixing bowl. In a separate bowl, cream the cup of butter and the sugar together until fluffy and light. Add the eggs one at a time, beating well after each addition—do not worry if the batter appears to curdle—that will not ruin the cake. Slowly beat in the dry ingredients alternately with the yogurt, lemon zest and lemon juice. Pour the batter into the pan. Bake 45 to 50 minutes.

While the cake cools in the pan for 15 minutes, make the Lemon Glaze (recipe below) To unmold the cake, put a plate on top of the Bundt pan and flip both over at the same time so the cake will slide right out. Put the glaze on while the cake is still warm.

LEMON GLAZE

½ cup freshly squeezed lemon juice
½ cup sugar
¼ cup water

Mix all ingredients in a small saucepan. Cook them over low heat without stirring until the sugar dissolves. Turn the heat up and swirl the pot, cooking until the mixture has become syrupy, about 10 to 12 minutes.

BANANA CAKE

SERVES
10 TO 12—
YIELDS
2 NINE-INCH
LAYERS

*T*his dense cake loaded with bananas, won't rise much. Don't be alarmed.

2¼ cups all-purpose flour
1½ teaspoon baking soda
 ½ teaspoon salt
 1 cup sweet butter
 1 cup sugar
 2 extra-large eggs
 1 teaspoon vanilla extract
 4 ripe bananas
 ¾ cup buttermilk
    Cream Cheese Frosting (page 242)
 ½ to 1 cup chopped pecans

(continued on next page)

Preheat the oven to 350 degrees.

Grease and flour 2 nine-inch round cake pans. Sift flour, baking powder and salt together. In a separate bowl, cream the butter and sugar until light and fluffy; add the eggs, then the vanilla extract. Mash 3 bananas in a separate bowl with a fork; add them to the butter-sugar mixture.

Fold the flour mixture into the banana mixture alternately with the buttermilk, ending with the dry ingredients. Divide the batter between the prepared pans.

Bake 30 to 35 minutes, until a toothpick inserted in the centers comes out clean. Cool in the pans 10 minutes, then turn out onto wire racks to cool completely.

Spread the top of 1 layer with ⅓ of the Cream Cheese Frosting. Make sure frosting is at room temperature. Slice the remaining banana in ½-inch circles and place the slices over the frosting; sprinkle with ¼ cup pecans. Top with the 2nd layer. Frost the sides and top of the cake with the remaining frosting and sprinkle ¼ to ½ cup pecans over the top.

CHOCOLATE APPLE CAKE

SERVES
10 TO 12—
YIELDS
2 NINE-INCH
LAYERS

*T*his cake calls for cocoa powder, apples, coffee and raisins. It sounds like a weird combination of ingredients, but when you think about it, they all go together naturally. This unusual dessert, when topped with whipped cream, makes a wonderful conclusion to any meal.

2¼ cups all-purpose flour	1½ cups sugar
1½ teaspoons baking powder	2 extra-large eggs
½ teaspoon salt	¾ cup brewed coffee
2 tablespoons Dutch cocoa powder	2 cups chopped apples
1 teaspoon ground cinnamon	1 cup golden raisins
¼ teaspoon ground nutmeg	1 cup heavy cream flavored with 1 teaspoon vanilla
¼ teaspoon ground cloves	and 2 tablespoons
1¾ cups sweet butter, softened	confectioner's sugar

Preheat oven to 350 degrees. Grease and flour 2 nine-inch round cake pans.

Sift together the flour, baking powder, salt, cocoa, cinnamon, nutmeg and cloves into medium bowl and set aside.

In a large bowl, cream butter and sugar until light and fluffy. Add the eggs 1 at a time, beating well after each addition. Add the dry ingredients alternately with the coffee, ending with the dry ingredients. Stir in the apples and raisins. Pour batter into the prepared pans.

Bake layers 30 to 35 minutes, until a toothpick inserted in the centers comes out clean. Cool 10 minutes in the pans, then turn out on wire racks to cool completely.

While cake layers are cooling, whip cream with vanilla and confectioner's sugar to soft peaks. Spread half the whipped cream on top of one layer. Place 2nd layer on top and frost with remaining whipped cream.

GERMAN CHOCOLATE CAKE

SERVES
10 TO 12—
YIELDS
3 NINE-INCH
LAYERS
FOR 1 CAKE

This very sweet chocolate cake, perhaps the most popular cake we serve, is coated with a caramel-colored cooked icing textured with pecans and shredded coconut.

    4 ounces sweet chocolate
2½ cups all-purpose flour
1½ teaspoons baking soda
  ¼ teaspoon salt
    1 cup sweet butter, softened
1½ cups sugar
    4 extra-large eggs, separated
    2 teaspoons vanilla extract
1¼ cups buttermilk
      Frosting (recipe follows)

Preheat oven to 350 degrees. Grease and flour 3 nine-inch round cake pans.

Melt the chocolate in a microwave, double boiler or *bain-marie* (see glossary for instructions), and set aside to cool.

Sift together the flour, baking soda and salt. In a separate bowl, cream the butter and sugar until light and fluffy. Add the egg yolks 1 at a time, beating well after each addition. Beat in the vanilla extract. Stir in the cooled chocolate and mix until incorporated.

Add dry ingredients alternately with buttermilk to chocolate mixture ending with the dry ingredients. In a glass or stainless steel bowl (don't use plastic or aluminum), beat the egg whites until they hold soft peaks but are not too stiff (they should be the consistency of the batter). Fold with rubber spoon ¼ of the egg whites into the batter, then fold in the remaining whites. Divide the batter among the prepared pans.

Bake 25 minutes, until the edges start to pull away from the sides of the pans and a toothpick inserted in the centers comes out clean. Cool 10 minutes in the pans, then turn the layers onto wire racks to cool completely.

Spread frosting on tops of layers only and stack the layers.

FROSTING FOR GERMAN CHOCOLATE CAKE

½ cup sweet butter, cubed
1 cup evaporated milk
½ cup firmly packed dark brown sugar
3 extra-large egg yolks, lightly beaten
1 teaspoon vanilla extract
1 cup sweetened, shredded coconut
1 cup pecan pieces

In a small saucepan, combine the butter, milk and sugar. Cook over low heat, stirring constantly. With a wooden spoon stir the mixture up from the bottom so the sugar does not scorch (do not whisk or the sugar will crystalize).

To temper egg yolks, stir a small amount of the heated mixture into the yolks. Slowly add the yolk mixture to the mixture in the pan, stirring constantly with a wooden spoon 12 to 15 minutes, or until mixture thickens (it should be the consistency of a milkshake and lightly coat the back of the spoon). Stir in vanilla extract and pour the frosting into a separate container to cool.

When mixture has cooled, stir in the coconut and pecans. Cool completely before frosting the cake.

CARROT CAKE

SERVES 10 TO 12—YIELDS 2 NINE-INCH LAYERS

Children adore this moist cake for an evening dessert or tucked into lunchboxes. You'll sneak pieces of it as an afternoon snack—it's that irresistible.

    1 cup whole wheat flour
    1 cup all-purpose flour
    2 teaspoons ground cinnamon
    1 teaspoon ground nutmeg
    ½ teaspoon salt
 1½ teaspoons baking soda
    ½ cup sweet butter, softened
    2 cups sugar
    ½ cup vegetable oil
    4 extra-large eggs
    2 teaspoons vanilla extract
    1 pound carrots, coarsely grated
       grated rind of 1 lemon
    ½ cup golden raisins
       Cream Cheese Frosting (page 242)

Preheat the oven to 350 degrees.

Grease and flour 2 nine-inch round cake pans. Combine the flours, cinnamon, nutmeg, salt and baking soda in a mixing bowl. In a separate bowl, cream the butter and sugar with a hand beater until light and fluffy. Add the oil and mix well. Add the eggs 1 at a time, beating well after each addition. Stir in the vanilla extract. Fold in the dry ingredients, then the carrots, raisins and lemon rind. Divide the batter between the pans.

Bake 25 to 30 minutes, or until a toothpick inserted in the centers of the layers comes out clean. Cool in the pans 10 minutes, then turn layers onto wire racks to cool completely. Frost top of each layer with Cream Cheese Frosting.

CREAM CHEESE FROSTING

We learned about our basic Cream Cheese Frosting from a former kitchen assistant; we then adjusted it to make it our own. It consists of cream cheese and powdered sugar, yet resembles a buttercream frosting in taste and texture. It is an uncomplicated, no-fail white frosting, so sturdy that it stands up well unrefrigerated and always retains its shine. We generally use this frosting on most of our cakes, unless otherwise indicated. It's so adaptable that you can change its flavor to suit any cake by adding cocoa, grated coconut, orange peel, or any flavoring you like.

    1 pound cream cheese
    ¾ cup sweet butter
    4 cups unsifted powdered sugar
    1 teaspoon vanilla extract
    1 teaspoon freshly squeezed lemon juice

Start with the cream cheese and butter at room temperature or the frosting will be lumpy. Place these in a large mixing bowl and, with a hand or electric beater, cream together well. Add the sugar slowly, beating until smooth. Add the vanilla and lemon juice and beat until thoroughly blended.

To frost, use a knife or spatula. Frost top and sides of cake, making sure frosting is at room temperature.

❖ ❖ ❖ ❖ ❖ ❖ ❖ ❖ ❖ ❖ ❖ ❖ ❖ ❖ ❖ ❖

The addition of your favorite frosting makes any cake just that much more delicious. Using a wax paper edge around the bottom of the cake allows you to frost without worrying about messing up your service plate. When frosting a layer cake, make sure the frosting is at room temperature. Spread frosting on bottom layer. Top with second layer. Spoon a generous amount of frosting on middle of top layer. With the flat side of the knife or *spatula, spread frosting over top and sides of cake. Using smooth, even strokes, smooth out sides of cake. Make decorative swirls on top. Remove wax paper collar and enjoy.*

❖ ❖ ❖ ❖ ❖ ❖ ❖ ❖ ❖ ❖ ❖ ❖ ❖ ❖ ❖ ❖

CHEESECAKE

A cross between a cake and a pie, this rich, dense dessert will please all cheesecake connoisseurs.

YIELDS
1 TEN-INCH
CHEESE-
CAKE
SERVES
10 TO 12

GRAHAM CRACKER CRUST

1½ cups graham cracker crumbs
¼ cup brown sugar
⅓ cup melted sweet butter

FILLING

2¼ pounds cream cheese, softened
1¼ cups sugar
5 extra-large eggs
6 tablespoons all-purpose flour
1½ cups sour cream
1 tablespoon grated lemon zest grated zest of 1 orange

Preheated oven to 325 degrees.

To prepare crust, combine crumbs, the ¼ cup sugar and the ⅓ cup melted butter. Pat into a 10-inch springform pan, pressing into bottom and 1 inch up sides of pan.

To make the filling, beat cream cheese on high speed in an electric mixer until soft. Gradually add 1¼ cups sugar. Turn mixer to low speed and add eggs 1 at a time, mixing well after each addition. Continuing on low speed, add flour until well incorporated. Mix in sour cream. Do not overbeat or the cheesecake will crack during baking. Stir in lemon and orange zest. Pour mixture into crust. Bake 1½ to 1¾ hours. Cheesecake is done when sides come away from pan edge and top is slightly brown and fairly firm.

Cookies and Other Morsels

A t any time of day, everyone loves homemade cookies—
1, 2, or better yet, a whole batch. Ours are big hand-
fuls, generous and moundy, and not oversweet. Baking cookies have the best aroma in the world, and when our ovens are
full of them, more people than usual seem to stop in to see
what we are making.

RASPBERRY CHOCOLATE RUGELACH

YIELDS
2 DOZEN

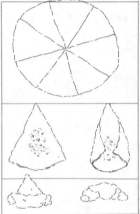

    3 cups all-purpose flour
 1½ cups sweet butter, softened
    1 extra-large egg yolk
    1 cup sour cream
  ¾ cup raspberry preserves
    2 tablespoons ground cinnamon
  ¾ cup chocolate chips
 1½ cups walnut pieces
    1 egg mixed with 1 tablespoon water
        confectioner's sugar

Place flour in a bowl, then cut in the butter until the mixture
resembles peas. Add the yolk and blend well. Stir in the sour
cream until well combined. Divide the dough into 3 balls, wrap
them in plastic wrap and refrigerate for 2 hours.

Preheat oven to 350 degrees. Line 9-by-12-inch cookie sheets
with parchment paper.

Lightly flour a board and rolling pin. Roll each ball into a 12-
inch circle of even thickness. Sprinkle each circle with 2 teaspoons
cinnamon, spread with ¼ cup raspberry preserves, and distribute
¼ cup chocolate chips and ½ cup walnut pieces on each circle. Cut
each into 4 equal squares, then cut each square into 2 equal triangles. Turn the corners of the wide edges in, then roll the wedges
from wide edge toward the point, tucking in the filling as you roll.
Curve slightly to shape into a crescent. Place each crescent on

lined cookie sheet point down and brush with egg wash.

Bake 20 minutes, until golden brown and slightly puffed. Cool on wire racks, then dust with confectioner's sugar.

ROCKY ROAD CHUBBS

12 TO 15 LARGE COOKIES

*W*e discovered, under the pressure of weekend business, how to melt chocolate fast. A loyal customer called one hectic Saturday afternoon to tell us she would be a half-hour late to pick up her order for brownies and cookies. We'd completely forgotten about the order, so we decided to try melting the chocolate in the microwave. Fortunately that worked beautifully and fast, and when the customer arrived to pick up her order, we handed her a box of hot treats. One of these was the Rocky Road Chubbs, a recipe inspired by Maida Heatter. These chewy mouthfuls are moundy blobs of baked chocolate mixed with pecans, chocolate chips, shredded coconut and marshmallows.

½ cup sweet butter
4 ounces unsweetened chocolate
8 ounces semisweet chocolate
4 extra-large eggs
2 cups sugar
2 teaspoons vanilla extract
⅔ cup all-purpose flour
½ teaspoon baking powder
1 cup pecan pieces
1 cup chocolate chips
1 cup large marshmallows, halved
2 cups shredded coconut

Preheat oven to 350 degrees.

Line 12-by-18-inch cookie sheets with parchment paper. Melt the butter and chocolates in a *bain-marie* (page 260) or whichever utensil you prefer. Set aside to cool.

In a mixing bowl, beat the eggs and sugar together with a wire whisk or an electric mixer until foamy. With a wooden spoon, stir in the vanilla extract, then the cooled chocolate. Add the flour and baking powder, stirring well. Stir in the pecans, chocolate chips, marshmallow halves and coconut. Place 3 tablespoons of dough 3 inches apart on the cookie sheets in large mounds about 2 inches wide. Bake 15 minutes or until shiny and firm. Let cool 10 minutes on cookie sheets, then remove cookies to wire racks to cool completely.

❖ ❖ ❖ ❖ ❖ ❖ ❖ ❖ ❖ ❖ ❖ ❖ ❖ ❖ ❖ ❖

We like soft, moundy, chewy cookies with moist insides. Cookie batter is not delicate but, once you add the flour, do not overbeat it. You can make the batter days ahead —and it is better when it is cold. You can even freeze it, if you wish. See individual cookie recipes for special tips.

❖ ❖ ❖ ❖ ❖ ❖ ❖ ❖ ❖ ❖ ❖ ❖ ❖ ❖ ❖ ❖

CHOCOLATE-DIPPED PECAN SHORTBREAD

YIELDS
8 ONE-INCH
WEDGES

We asked ourselves jokingly one day what special cookie we could invent that would make us famous. We decided it might be a shortbread cookie based on a recipe Carrie—wrapped from toe to thigh in a plaster cast—had concocted one rainy afternoon at home, when she cut up warm shortbread and dipped its corners into melted chocolate, then into pecans.

1½ cups all-purpose flour
½ cup sugar
½ cup ground pecans (¼ pound pecan meats)
10½ tablespoons sweet butter, softened
3 ounces semisweet chocolate
½ cup toasted shredded coconut (optional)

Preheat oven to 350 degrees.

Combine the flour, sugar and pecans in a mixing bowl. Cut in the butter until the mixture stays together when pressed. Shortbread should be worked lightly so it will taste the way the name suggests—short (buttery). Press the dough into a 9-inch round pan; score lightly with a knife into 8 equal wedges (do not cut all the way through), then prick the dough with a fork in even rows on top of each wedge.

Bake 30 minutes, or until the top is light brown. Cool, then separate the wedges completely with a knife. Cool thoroughly. Remove the wedges from the pan by flipping them over onto the bottom of another pan; remove and place on a wire rack to cool completely. Handle them gently so they won't break. Meanwhile, melt the chocolate in the *bain-marie* (see page 260) or a microwave or a double boiler. When the shortbread is completely cool, dip each pointed end into the chocolate. Place the wedges on a sheet of parchment paper or on a rack set over aluminum foil, sprinkle on coconut, if using, and let chocolate harden.

CHOCOLATE CHIP PEANUT COOKIES

YIELDS
12 LARGE
COOKIES

These are sensational—all the yummy cookie tastes we loved as children.

½ cup sweet butter, melted
¾ cup firmly packed brown sugar
¼ cup granulated sugar
1 extra-large egg
¾ cup all-purpose flour
½ teaspoon salt
1 teaspoon baking powder
½ teaspoon ground cinnamon
¼ teaspoon ground nutmeg
1¼ cups old-fashioned rolled oats
⅓ cup unsalted peanuts
⅓ cup chocolate chips

Preheat oven to 350 degrees. Line two 12-by-18-inch cookie sheets with parchment paper.

Beat the butter and the sugars in a mixing bowl until creamy. Beat in the egg. In a separate bowl, sift the flour, salt, baking powder, cinnamon and nutmeg. Stir by tablespoonfuls into the butter mixture, mixing well after each addition. Stir in the oats, peanuts and chocolate chips.

Mound the dough by large tablespoonfuls 2 inches apart onto the cookies sheets. Bake 15 minutes. Remove to wire racks to cool completely.

LEMON BARS

YIELDS

16

We can't think of a single person who hasn't fallen in love with these lemon morsels that resemble a lemon meringue pie minus the meringue.

TOPPING

2 cups all-purpose flour	4 extra-large eggs, lightly beaten
½ cup sugar	2 cups sugar
1 cup sweet butter,	5 tablespoons all-purpose flour
softened	¼ cup lemon juice
	grated rind of 1 lemon
	confectioner's sugar

Preheat oven to 350 degrees. Line an 11-by-18-inch baking pan with parchment, cutting the corners so they fit nicely.

Combine the 2 cups of flour and ½ cup of sugar in a mixing bowl, then add the butter, working the mixture with your hands until the dough is well blended and smooth. Pat the dough ¼ inch thick onto the bottom of the pan, and ½ inch up the sides to form a rim. Bake 15 minutes, or until the dough is light golden.

Meanwhile, make the topping: Lightly beat eggs with the 2 cups of sugar in a mixing bowl with a wooden spoon (the top will become crusty if overbeaten). Add the 5 tablespoons of flour, 1 tablespoon at a time, mixing each just until incorporated. Mix in the lemon juice and rind. Spread the mixture over the baked crust, return it to the oven, and bake 15 to 20 minutes longer, until the topping is set and the crust is light brown. Remove from the oven and cool in the pan.

Cut in pan into 2-by-2¾-inch bars. When cooled, dust with confectioner's sugar and take out of pan with spatula. Peel off of parchment paper.

6

LEFTOVERS

*I*n a recent newspaper interview, three top New York chefs
agreed on the characteristics of a fine cook: He or she could
chop an onion, roast a chicken and creatively use up leftovers
from your refrigerator.

A leftover can be anything, or many things crowded and stacked
together on the refrigerator shelf. Boiled potatoes. Salad remnants.
Half a cup of gravy. A surplus from a bountiful garden. A foil pack
from last night's restaurant dinner. The deliberate extra portions
made ahead for quick reheating. Any sensible and practical cook
knows better than to discard leftovers. At least not immediately—
not until the week has passed and he or she still has not figured
out how to use up those aging morsels.

The leftover dilemma looms large in most family kitchens, but
can easily be solved. First, erase any bad connotations leftovers
may have in your mind. They deserve the same respect you would
give any other food. Then, remember that leftovers are not the
lazy way out of cooking. That would be like wearing an unironed
dress or shirt to work. Using leftovers is still like composing a
standard dinner menu, but the advantage with leftovers is that you
are starting with some portion of the meal already cooked. If the
food had been handled, cooked and stored well, it will remain
delectable through its second appearance at the table.

We have devoted this entire chapter to leftovers. As practical
cooks, we cannot stand to throw out unused foods, and we have
learned through experience how to recycle last night's filet mignon
for steak sandwiches, vegetables for a salad or soup, and shellfish
for yet another wholesome meal. Our leftover ideas incorporate
foods from recipes in this book. But maybe we will inspire you to
think of your leftovers in your own creative way.

Meat

BEEF

1. Leftover beef stew can easily be turned into a beef pot pie by adding cubed fresh vegetables to the beef and its gravy, and sealing ingredients with a piecrust seasoned with herbs.

2. Leftover roast beef can be cubed and added to our Vegetable Chowder (page 49).

3. Use leftover beef filet for an elegant sesame beef salad by combining thin strips of beef with assorted vegetables such as snow peas, sliced carrots, sliced mushrooms, sliced scallions, cubed potatoes or sliced cucumbers, dressed with a creamy sesame oil and soy sauce vinaigrette blended together like a mayonnaise, and enriched with whole eggs or egg yolks. If you wish, add shrimp or other seafood to the salad.

4. For an open-faced steak sandwich, slice filet or roast beef, then quickly sauté. Place a few slices on a slice of French bread, and spread it with our Mustard Horseradish Sauce (see page 211). Serve with a tomato and avocado salad.

5. Slice filet, then julienne the sliced meat in the same marinade used for the salmon dinner, Chapter IV, page 177. Then make a salad by combining the meat with little chunks of Parmesan cheese, arugula and radicchio and dressing everything with a walnut vinaigrette.

6. Sliced leftover pot roast makes a delicious brisket barbecue sandwich; or, instead of a sandwich, top the brisket slices with sauerkraut heated with champagne and mustard, and serve with a potato salad.

HAM, FRESH, AND PORK

1. Always a perfect sandwich filling, sliced fresh ham can be dressed up for the fancy French Croque Monsieur, a sandwich of sliced ham-and-cheese made with French bread and topped with a white sauce; and, for Croque Madame, the same combination with added tomato slices. The whole sandwich is dipped in beaten egg and fried on both sides, like French toast. White sauce is then added on top. Alternatively, sliced ham can be used for a peasant-type combination of ham, grated Gruyère and Parmesan layered on a sliced and buttered loaf of French bread brushed with mustard. Place this open-faced sandwich on a baking sheet and then

under a broiler until the cheese melts and browns slightly. Serve any of these sandwiches with a warm potato salad.

2. For an elegant Sunday dinner entree, in a baking dish poach trimmed and cleaned Belgian endive in a milk-water mixture for 15 to 20 minutes, or until almost soft. Remove from the liquid and drain. Thinly slice ham and Gruyère and wrap around the endive, put wrapped endive again into the baking dish, cover with white sauce and sprinkle with Parmesan. Dot mixture with butter and bake until golden. Serve with a watercress or mâche salad.

3. Julienne the meat from leftover pork chops or pork roast and use it in a stir-fry with sliced carrots, scallions, zucchini, shredded Chinese cabbage, snow peas and broccoli florets. If you have cold leftover white or brown rice, add this also. In a small mixing bowl, combine soy sauce. chopped fresh ginger, minced garlic and ground white pepper. Heat vegetable oil in a wok, stir-fry the pork, vegetables and rice, and just before scooping them out of the wok, stir in the soy sauce mixture.

4. For a simple sandwich, slice a firm roll or loaf of French bread in half, spread each half with ketchup or mustard, then layer the bread with sliced pork and Brie and, for crunch, add mâche or watercress.

5. Heat leftovers of the Paprika Pork Roast (page 94), then serve it with a salad of equal amounts of cooked and cooled red potatoes and peeled, seeded and sliced cucumber, mixed with sour cream, snipped dill, lemon juice, vinegar, olive oil, mayonnaise, salt, pepper and a pinch of sugar.

LAMB

1. To make a mock moussaka—the Greek baked lamb-and-eggplant casserole—cube any leftover roast lamb and set aside. Allowing half an eggplant per person, slice eggplant in half lengthwise, then into ½-inch-thick slices. Degorge it (see glossary), dip the slices into beaten egg, then into bread crumbs seasoned with herbs, salt and pepper. Sauté slices in olive oil until they are browned. Allowing half a beefsteak tomato per person, slice tomato in half, and cook as in Stuffed Chicken Breast, page 154. Make a white sauce enriched with wine, layer the meat, eggplant and tomatoes in a casserole, cover with sauce, then a sprinkling of feta cheese, and bake in a 350-degree oven until bubbly.

2. For a unique lamb salad, follow directions for Veal Salad, page 67, but use lamb instead; or add cubed lamb to a Provençal mixture of tomato, olives, garlic, olive oil, capers, anchovies (optional), seasoned with mustard vinaigrette.

3. For a lamb sandwich, slice lamb from roast and set aside. Slice a half-loaf of French bread in half lengthwise, then layer on it chopped tomatoes or our Tomato Concasse (page 150), the lamb, and crumbled feta cheese. Serve this with a crisp spinach and red onion salad dressed with olive oil, vinegar and minced garlic.

MEATLOAF

1. Mash cooked meatloaf, sauté it like ground beef, then spoon into a baking dish. Then sauté onion slices in butter seasoned with spices. Stir in ketchup or mustard to taste, and spoon the onion mixture over the meatloaf. Sprinkle this mixture with grated Cheddar cheese, then place dish under the broiler until the cheese melts.

2. Or, for a meatloaf sandwich, slice the meatloaf, place on a buttered slice of French bread, top with the onion mixture as above, place on a baking sheet, then place sheet under the broiler until the cheese melts.

Poultry

CHICKEN

Unused cooked chicken breasts from any of our recipes can be frozen until needed. For a quick and unusual poultry main course, thaw the breasts, deep-fry them and serve crisp breasts on a waffle with a side dish of cole slaw or creamed corn.

Otherwise, leftover cooked chicken breasts or cold roast chicken can be used in the following ways:

1. Make a chicken salad with cut-up fresh mango, grapes and sliced avocado, dressed with an orange-flavored mayonnaise made by adding orange juice and grated orange zest to our basic mayonnaise (page 63). Garnish the salad with mushrooms, scallions and cucumbers, all sliced.

2. Reheat chicken breasts by roasting them in a 375-degree oven with butter, white wine, salt and pepper. Remove them from the oven, cut them into narrow strips, and place on sliced French bread. Cover all with barbecue sauce and grated Cheddar cheese and slide under a broiler for 3 minutes. Cook until the cheese melts and is bubbly. Serve with French fries or fried onion rings.

3. Wrap uncooked chicken breasts around a filling of cut-up dried prunes and apricots and sliced carrots. Or, instead of carrots, use seedless green grapes. Serve the breasts with a cream sauce.

DUCK AND GOOSE

Cooks are often puzzled about what to do with leftovers from these birds. They need not be. You can use leftovers from either bird for the first 3 recipes, and duck meat for the fourth.

1. Remove meat from the carcass, leaving skin on, and julienne it. Roast hot Italian sausages, sliced into ½-inch-thick rounds, in a 350-degree oven until crisp, about 20 minutes. Reheat the julienned duck or goose meat with the sausages for 5 or 6 minutes. While the sausages cook, either warm up leftover mashed potatoes, or prepare fresh. Sauté sliced apples and onions (page 98). To serve, top the mashed potatoes with the meats and then the apple-onion mixture.

2. Remove meat from the carcass, taking the skin off, and mince finely for a hash. Set aside. Make Hash Browns (page 42), substituting the meat for half the amount of potatoes. Fry in butter and, if you wish, add cubed cooked beets.

3. Remove meat from the carcass, then julienne or cube it. Heat vegetable oil in a wok and stir-fry the meat with snow peas and shredded Chinese cabbage. Serve this mixture with Apple Fritters (page 141).

4. With leftover duck meat we make a delicious lemon duck salad inspired by our Lemon Chicken. Remove duck meat from the carcass, leaving skin on, and julienne the meat. Place it in a large mixing bowl. To that add very thinly sliced lemons, sliced scallions, cleaned, blanched snow peas and peeled, sliced Granny Smith apples. Dress the salad with a sprinkle of lemon juice stirred into mayonnaise. Serve on a bed of red-leaf lettuce.

TURKEY

1. Leftover roast turkey can be used for a hot turkey sandwich. Lightly toast two slices of white or rye bread. Place them on a baking sheet with a mound of leftover stuffing on each slice, then layer slices of white and dark meat on top of the stuffing. Spoon a generous portion of gravy over top and bake in a 325-degree oven for 15 to 20 minutes. Serve immediately with a garnish of cranberry relish.

2. Leftover cooked turkey can also be cubed for a Pot Pie (page 151), or minced, mixed with eggs and bread crumbs, formed into patties, sautéed, and served with relish, sautéed kale or Creamed Dilled Peas (page 196).

Seafood

Because all seafood is highly perishable, plan to use any as leftovers within a day or 2 of serving the original dish.

ANY FIRM WHITE FISH

Dip raw fish fillets or steaks into a buttermilk-egg batter, then into seasoned flour. In a skillet, sauté the fish in butter and oil. Drain on paper towels, then sandwich in a roll or dill bread, and serve with a potato salad.

MUSSELS AND CLAMS

Unless you can buy an exact amount of loose mussels and clams, you will have leftovers of any prepacked mussels and clams used in the recipes in section "Seafood Meals" beginning on page 157. This dinner suggestion is a perfect example of our combined European and American backgrounds: steamed shellfish served with fried potatoes. Clean the shellfish, cut up mature potatoes for frying and chop leeks, onions, celery and garlic. Add the vegetables to a large stockpot with white wine, half that amount of water, salt and pepper. Season this with thyme and bay leaf. Cook all this over very low heat for 10 to 15 minutes. Add the clams. Turn on the heat under the oil, and start frying the potatoes, but do not overcrowd the pot. As they finish cooking, place them in a bowl with paper toweling for draining, then sprinkle with salt to taste. After the clams have steamed a few moments, add the mussels and cook another 10 minutes or until they all open. Discard any that do not open. Serve mussels and clams in one big bowl and potatoes in another. If you wish, prepare Tartar Sauce (page 85) for dipping fries.

SHRIMP OR SCALLOPS

1. For a light luncheon salad, combine any leftover cooked shrimp or scallops with julienned cooked chicken breast, sliced mushrooms, broccoli florets, snow peas, carrots and cucumbers, and dress with a dill mayonnaise. Serve on a bed of leaf lettuce, or in half an avocado.

2. Mince raw shrimp and chicken and combine with leftover mashed potatoes seasoned with 1 tablespoon Parmesan cheese per pound of shrimp and chicken combined. Follow our Codfish Cake recipe (page 188) using the leftover mashed potatoes to bind the ingredients together. Form the mixture into a sausage shape, wrap in wax paper and chill for 2 hours. Remove from refrigerator and slice into 1-inch-thick slices. Dip each into beaten egg, then into seasoned bread crumbs. In a large skillet, fry patties in a combination of oil and butter. Drain on paper toweling and serve with a dill mayonnaise and a tart salad such as radicchio and endive.

3. For an unusual sandwich, serve butterflied cooked shrimp with Pea Salad (page 129), all layered on a roll and spread with barbecue sauce.

4. Hollow out a beefsteak tomato and stuff with chopped cooked shrimp mixed with mayonnaise. Serve on a bed of spinach or lettuce, drizzle all with a vinaigrette sauce, and sprinkle with garlic croutons (over the spinach only).

SWORDFISH

Cube leftovers and slide onto a skewer for shish kebabs, using with the fish such fruits as pineapple, kiwi, papaya or mango, and red peppers. Marinate the kebabs in a mixture of soy sauce, lemon juice, vegetable oil and salt and pepper. Broil briefly and serve with brown rice mixed with roasted pecans.

Vegetables

ASPARAGUS

Cold, cooked asparagus spears can be cut into thirds lengthwise, and used in a stir-fry dish, or added to a chicken and pasta salad dressed with our *Rouille* (page 168).

BROCCOLI

In a wok, in vegetable oil, stir-fry raw or cooked broccoli florets and trimmed stems with julienned red peppers, sesame seeds, soy sauce, grated fresh ginger and rice vinegar.

CABBAGE

Shred raw cabbage leaves and mix them in a bowl with thinly sliced onions, teaspoonfuls of butter, champagne or rosé wine for moistness, cubed apples, pears, pineapple and/or orange or tangerine sections. Layer in a baking dish, and sprinkle with brown sugar, salt, pepper and anise seeds. Stirring regularly, bake in a 350-degree oven for 30 minutes.

CARROTS, GLAZED

For a light summer soup with a gingery zest, use a chicken or vegetable stock. Sauté sliced onions, garlic, and fresh, sliced ginger, then deglaze the skillet with white wine. Add all ingredients to the stock and simmer until softened. Just before serving, add the glazed carrots and cook until heated through. Sprinkle a pinch of nutmeg over the soup just before ladling into soup bowls, and garnish each bowl with a sprig of mint. Pass a bowl of whipped cream, heavy cream or *crème fraiche* for stirring into the soup.

KALE

Oven-braise a large portion of leftover raw kale in a baking dish with chicken stock and lemon juice (or white or red wine), butter, cubed bacon and salt and pepper. Braise in a 350-degree oven for 20 minutes. If you have only a few leaves of kale, deep-fry them and use as plate garnish.

MUSHROOMS

1. For a stuffing mixture, chop raw mushrooms and mix them with chopped onions and parsley. Wrap a chicken breast around mixture or stuff it under chicken skin, or mound mixture into mushroom caps, or stir mixture with melted butter and spread it over top of a roast beef. Or spread under any cut of meat to add extra flavor when braising.

2. Marinate large mushroom caps in olive oil, lemon juice, dried herbs, salt and pepper for half an hour, stirring frequently to coat well. Then on an oven-top griddle, grill the mushrooms and serve them with roasted red peppers, or as a side dish with grilled meats, or added to a salad.

POTATOES, MASHED

Versatile mashed potatoes can be used up many different, interesting ways.

1. With a tablespoon, scoop up cold mashed potatoes and roll into 1-inch balls. Dip the balls into beaten egg, then roll in seasoned bread crumbs and grated Parmesan cheese. Chill until firm, then bake or deep-fry them until golden.

2. To make a *gratinée*, moisten the cold mashed potatoes with enough milk or heavy cream so they are soft. Then butter a baking dish and sprinkle it with grated Parmesan cheese. Add the potatoes, patting them down until layer is of uniform thickness; striate the surface with the tines of a fork. Sprinkle the surface with paprika, grated Cheddar cheese and dabs of butter and bake in a 375-degree oven till golden.

3. "Bubble and Squeak," a popular British dish, is perfect for leftover mashed potatoes. To make, stir any leftover vegetables into the mashed potatoes (which may need moistening with warmed milk) in a mixing bowl. In a skillet, heat butter till bubbly, then spread in the potato-vegetable mixture and flatten it like a pancake. Cook over medium heat and flip over when underside is golden. Brown second side. This mixture literally squeaks as it

cooks, hence the name.

4. Instead of flour, use leftover mashed potatoes to thicken a winter soup made of chicken or vegetable stock. In separate batches, fry the mashed potatoes with chopped onions, chopped celery and sliced leeks. Add these to stock and simmer till heated through and thickened. For extra richness add heavy cream. Garnish the soup with garlic croutons.

RICE AND WILD RICE

Cold brown, white or wild rice makes an excellent salad when dressed with an herbed mayonnaise, to be served with cold poached chicken or salmon.

SPINACH, CREAMED

1. This quickly converts to an unusual chicken stuffing. Combine the creamed spinach with grated cheese and diced tomatoes. Then, split an uncooked roasting chicken in half lengthwise and pull back the skin on each half. Slide your hand between the skin and the flesh and stuff this pocket with the creamed spinach mixture. Over the skin, drizzle melted butter mixed with salt, pepper, vinegar and a pinch of sugar and roast for 30 to 40 minutes in a 350-degree oven.

2. Mix creamed spinach with the ricotta cheese mixture we make for our Vegetarian Lasagna (page 59). Stuff this into cooked pasta shells, layer in a baking dish, cover with tomato sauce and sprinkle with mozzarella and Parmesan cheese. Bake at 350 degrees till bubbly and brown. Serve with garlic bread.

SQUASH, ACORN

Remove the skin and scoop out seeds, then puree squash, moistening it with orange juice, and seasoning with a sprinkle of cinnamon and nutmeg.

ZUCCHINI

Add cubed raw or cooked zucchini to Tomato Concasse (page 150). Or slice raw zucchini, dip slices in beer, then in a mixture of grated Parmesan cheese, bread crumbs, paprika, dry mustard, salt and pepper, and deep-fry the slices at 375 degrees. Raw zucchini can be added to a relish or stir-fried with other vegetables.

Miscellaneous

BISCUITS

Split the biscuits across and use the halves as a base for creamed chicken, turkey or beef. And, of course, these are delicious for fruit shortcake. Use seasonal fresh fruit or a combination of fruits, and wash and chill them. Whip heavy cream sweetened with powdered sugar and vanilla. Split the biscuits across; warm them if they seem a little hard. Top each half with a portion of fruit, then whipped cream.

VEGETARIAN CHILI

Heat and serve leftover chili in individual bowls, topping each portion with canned corn kernels and ketchup. This resembles a Sloppy Joe in a bowl. Or spoon heated chili over freshly cooked pasta, and sprinkle grated Monterey Jack cheese over each serving. Or use the chili to stuff under the skin of half a roast chicken (see directions for stuffing under Creamed Spinach (page 172). Lay the stuffed uncooked chicken halves on a baking sheet. Mix melted butter, wine vinegar, pinch of sugar, salt and pepper, and brush on chicken skin. Cook for 15 minutes, then reduce temperature to 350 degrees and continue cooking another 30 minutes. Serve with our Pea Salad (page 129)

GLOSSARY

BAIN-MARIE: A water bath for gentle cooking or heating. Like a double boiler, this consists of a container half filled with hot water in which another container filled with food sits. This arrangement either cooks or keeps food warm at a constant low temperature.

BEURRE MANIE: A superlative thickener for sauces and gravies. Combine equal amounts of room-temperature butter and flour and rub them between your thumb and second finger to form tiny droplets, allowing them to fall into the saucepan. Use only at the last moment, and never allow them to boil.

Butterflying shrimp: Devein the shrimp (discussed on page 158), but make a deeper incision, almost cutting the shrimp in half. When you open it up, it will be flat and have the shape of a butterfly, hence the name.

Chiffonade: To make these slender ribbons of fresh herbs and leafy greens such as spinach and lettuce, roll up the leaves, then julienne them very thin.

Degorge: To remove bitter seeds and juices from such vegetables as zucchini and eggplant, sprinkle slices of these vegetables with kosher salt, and allow them to sit for 15 minutes. Then, rinse the salt off and squeeze the slices with your hands, patting them dry with paper towels.

FUMET: The French word for fish stock made from butter, a selection of vegetables for seasonings and fish bones and trimmings. These are cooked together gently to extract maximum flavor; the resultant broth can be used alone or as the base for soups or stews.

· ◇ · ◇ · ◇ · ◇ · ◇ · ◇ · ◇ · ◇ · ◇

HERBES DE PROVENCE: If you could take a train ride to the south of France and bottle its fragrance, it would smell like *herbes de Provence*. Actually, these are a combination, in equal portions, of rosemary, thyme, sage and basil. Use fresh or dried.

Julienne: To cut food into matchstick-sized pieces.

LIAISON: A thickener of egg yolks only, whipped with heavy cream, both at room temperature to prevent curdling when they are combined with a hot sauce. Take a ladleful of whatever needs thickening and drizzle it into a bowl containing the *liaison*. Then turn the heat very low, whisk a ladleful of this mixture into the pot, then whisk in the remaining *liaison*. Never let it boil or it will curdle.

Proof: Letting warm water sit with yeast and a pinch of sugar, in a bowl, till the mixture foams.

ROUX: Used to thicken sauces and gravies, this is a mixture of flour and fat heated gently for a few minutes before being added to the sauce or gravy.

SAUTOIR: A deep pan like a skillet, for sautéing foods.

Sweat: To cook vegetables in butter or oil over low heat until they are soft and translucent but not brown.

TOURNEE: To pare a potato from one end to the other to obtain 7 uniform flat surfaces. To perform, hold the potato in one hand, and the paring knife in the other. Slice off the top and the bottom, then rotate the potato after each lengthwise slice.

INDEX

About the Authors

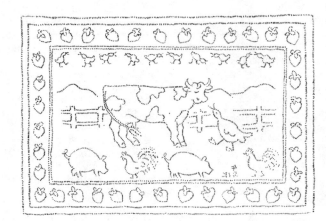

Carrie Levin's formal culinary training began at Leith's School of Food and Wine in London. In 1979 she moved back to the United States, worked briefly at The Russian Tea Room and subsequently began an internship at The Four Seasons, under Chef Seppi Renggli, whom she considers her principal mentor and inspiration. In spite of her background of sophisticated European cuisine, Carrie's true desire—which she has fulfilled at the Good Enough to Eat restaurants—is to create a simpler fare, similar to the peasant food of the south of France, but American in character. Carrie lives in New York City with her husband, William Perley.

Contrary to what anyone who has eaten her food thinks, Ann Nickinson has had no formal training. She was brought up in a home where food was taken very seriously, and that attitude has been carried with her to Good Enough to Eat. Ann began her culinary career cooking and selling food wholesale from her home. As her clientele grew, she entered the catering business, its expansion resulting in the founding of Good Enough to Eat. Ann would like someday to dedicate herself full-time to the operation of a country inn where she can be with her dogs, cats and cows and make her customers happy. Ann lives in New York City.